Quantum Internet

A Simple Guide to Big Ideas

Nova Martian

Contents

Chapter 1

Understanding Quantum Basics

This foundational chapter introduces the core principles of quantum mechanics required for the quantum internet. We begin with the historical emergence of quantum theory and its departure from classical physics, then describe how quantum states are represented and evolve. Next, we examine the peculiar phenomena of superposition and probability amplitudes, followed by the profound implications of entanglement. Finally, we explore how measurement collapses quantum states and illustrate these ideas with the double-slit experiment, preparing the reader for quantum information and communication.

1.1 Introduction to Quantum Physics

At the dawn of the 20th century, physics found itself at a crossroads. The classical mechanics championed by Isaac Newton—a majestic framework that had explained everything from falling apples to planetary orbits with astounding precision—began to show its cracks. Experiments probing the microscopic world of atoms and light yielded puzzling results that classical theories could not explain. This intellectual unrest gave birth to quantum physics, a revolutionary theory that reshaped our understanding of nature's fundamental workings.

1

The origins of quantum theory trace back to two perplexing phenomena: blackbody radiation and the photoelectric effect. Classical physics predicted that a heated object should emit electromagnetic radiation with a continuous spectrum growing without bound at shorter wavelengths, leading to the so-called "ultraviolet catastrophe." In 1900, Max Planck resolved this by proposing that energy is not radiated smoothly but rather in discrete packets, or *quanta*, each proportional to the frequency f of the radiation. This bold hypothesis, expressed as

$$E = hf,$$

where h (Planck's constant) is a fixed fundamental number, marked the first step in quantum thinking. Soon after, Albert Einstein explained the photoelectric effect—where light shone on metal ejects electrons—by treating light itself as composed of discrete quanta called photons, confirming that energy quantization was not just a mathematical trick but a fundamental aspect of reality.

Classical mechanics, with its elegantly deterministic laws, imagined the universe as a perfectly clockwork system: knowing the initial positions and velocities of particles allowed one to predict their future trajectories precisely. In stark contrast, quantum physics introduced an intrinsic probabilistic nature to the microscopic realm. Instead of a particle having a definite position and momentum simultaneously, quantum theory proposes that the state of a particle is fundamentally described by probabilities—a radical shift from certainty to uncertainty. This shift dismantles the comforting predictability of Newton's world and replaces it with a universe wherein only the likelihood of an outcome can be forecast.

Behind this profound change lies a new mathematical framework built on a few fundamental postulates. First, the state of a quantum system is represented by a vector in a complex vector space called *Hilbert space*. Think of these state vectors as encoding all that can be known about a system, though this knowledge is inherently probabilistic rather than definite. Second, a system's evolution over time—how this state vector changes—is governed by *unitary transformations*, which ensure probabilities remain consistent throughout dynamic processes. Lastly, measurement plays a special role: it doesn't simply reveal a pre-existing property but probabilistically *collapses* the state into one of several possible outcomes, with the wavefunction's predictive power realized only in these probabilities.

To grasp the concept of state vectors more concretely, imagine an electron not as a tiny billiard ball with a clearly defined position, but as a vector residing within a vast mathematical space. This space is complex, meaning it includes numbers involving the square root of negative one, which might seem abstract. Yet, this complexity is necessary to capture the oscillatory and wave-like behaviors observed in experiments. Each vector's direction encodes the electron's state, while its length corresponds to the probability amplitude, whose squared magnitude gives the probability that a measurement will yield a specific result.

One of quantum theory's striking revelations is the quantization of energy levels within atoms. Unlike the continuous allowed energies of classical orbits, electrons inhabit discrete energy states. This explains why atomic spectra—the characteristic lines of colored light emitted or absorbed by atoms—appear as sharp, well-defined lines rather than a smooth rainbow. Each spectral line corresponds to an electron's leap between quantized energy levels, emitting or absorbing energy exactly equal to hf in the process. This discovery not only confirmed Planck's bold hypothesis but also provided a detailed map of atomic structure.

Complementing these ideas is the principle of *wave–particle duality*. Early in the 20th century, experiments revealed an astonishing duality: particles such as electrons exhibit both particle-like and wave-like characteristics. Electrons can produce interference patterns—telltale signs of waves—yet they also impact detectors as individual localized dots, reflecting their particle nature. Louis de Broglie encapsulated this in his famous relation:

$$\lambda = \frac{h}{p},$$

where λ is the wavelength associated with a particle and p is its momentum. This formula bridges the classical distinction between waves and particles, showing that everything possesses a wavelength inversely proportional to its momentum. For macroscopic objects this wavelength is unimaginably tiny, which is why classical physics remains a superb approximation at everyday scales.

Central to the quantum description is the *superposition principle*. Unlike classical states that must uniquely choose one configuration, quantum states can combine linearly to form new, profoundly richer states. For instance, an electron can simultaneously exist in multiple locations or spin states until a measurement forces a definite outcome. This principle underlies much of the strangeness and power of quantum theory and serves as the foundation for emerging technologies such as quantum computing.

The radical departure from classical intuitions embodied in these developments has not merely remained a theoretical curiosity. Quantum physics underpins technologies integral to modern life: lasers, transistors, magnetic resonance imaging, and even the emerging promise of quantum cryptography. Yet, beyond practical applications, quantum theory challenges us to reconsider the very nature of reality, measurement, and information.

As we proceed, we will delve deeper into fascinating consequences of quantum principles such as qubits, which extend the notion of classical bits into superpositions; entanglement, where particles become mysteriously correlated across distances; and the nuanced role of measurement that transcends the simple notion of observation. These ideas, born from the early quantum insights outlined here, continue to inspire both philosophical debate and cutting-edge innovation, inviting us to explore a universe more subtle, surprising, and beautiful than classical physics ever allowed.

1.2 Qubits versus Classical Bits

At the heart of classical computing lies the bit, a humble yet powerful entity representing information as either a 0 or a 1. This binary system, simple in concept, forms the foundation for all classical logic and computation. A classical bit is a two-valued variable: it definitely exists in one of two distinct states, with no ambiguity. Each bit can be thought of as a tiny switch, firmly fixed in either an "off" (0) or "on" (1) position. This discrete on/off nature makes classical bits easy to understand, manipulate, and store reliably across myriad electronic and mechanical devices.

Quantum computing, however, challenges this fundamental notion by introducing the qubit, or quantum bit, which generalizes and transcends the classical bit. Unlike its classical counterpart, a qubit does not settle for being just a 0 or a 1. Instead, it

5

flourishes in a world of possibility, existing in a delicate balance known as *superposition*—a combination of both states simultaneously. This is not mere ambiguity or uncertainty in the classical sense but a genuine, physical coexistence, a hallmark of quantum mechanics that fundamentally reshapes how we think about information.

Mathematically, the state of a qubit can be expressed as

$$|\psi\rangle = \alpha|0\rangle + \beta|1\rangle,$$

where the kets $|0\rangle$ and $|1\rangle$ denote the two classical basis states, and the complex numbers α and β are the probability amplitudes corresponding to each. These amplitudes contain all the measurable information about the system and must satisfy the normalization condition

$$|\alpha|^2 + |\beta|^2 = 1,$$

ensuring that the total probability of finding the qubit in either state upon measurement is unity.

This elegant expression conceals a vast richness: the qubit's state space is continuous and multidimensional, in direct contrast to the discrete binary of classical bits. Visualizing this space is facilitated by the *Bloch sphere*, a geometric representation where any pure qubit state maps onto a point on the unit sphere's surface. The north and south poles correspond to the classical states $|0\rangle$ and $|1\rangle$, but every other point represents a unique superposition. The angles parameterizing this sphere capture the relative weights and phases of α and β. This sphere becomes a playground for understanding quantum operations as rotations, vividly illustrating how qubits can smoothly transition among an infinite spectrum of states, rather than flipping merely between two fixed positions.

An essential nuance in this quantum picture is the role of *coherence*, which refers to the preservation of the relative phase between $|0\rangle$ and $|1\rangle$ in a superposition. Qubits maintain coherence by prospectively evolving in this quantum state space, but interactions with the surrounding environment can disrupt this delicate balance—a phenomenon known as *decoherence*. Decoherence effectively collapses the coherent superposition into a classical probabilistic mixture, erasing the uniquely quantum information encoded in relative phases and undermining the power of quantum computation. Maintaining coherence is one of the paramount challenges in building functional quantum processors and requires extreme isolation or active error correction strategies.

Physically, realizing qubits demands harnessing quantum systems that naturally exhibit two-level dynamics. Diverse platforms have been explored with varying advantages. Trapped ions, isolated and manipulated with lasers, offer exquisite control and long coherence times. Superconducting circuits, fabricated with advanced lithography, provide scalability and fast gate operations. Other realizations include quantum dots, nitrogen-vacancy centers in diamond, and photons. Despite their differences, each platform embodies the qubit's defining trait: the ability to inhabit and evolve within a quantum superposition, governed by the laws of quantum mechanics.

The profound divergence between classical bits and qubits is well captured in the following comparison:

Feature	Classical Bit	Qubit
State Space	Discrete: either 0 or 1	Continuous: superpositions of $|0\rangle$ and $|1\rangle$
Information Representation	Deterministic single value	Probabilistic amplitudes with phase
Measurement Outcome	Definite 0 or 1	Collapses probabilistically to 0 or 1
Superposition	Absent	Fundamental
Entanglement	None	Possible, enabling non-classical correlations
Physical Realization	Transistors, magnetic domains	Trapped ions, superconducting loops, photons
Error Sensitivity	Low, stable states	High, susceptible to decoherence

Table 1.1: Comparison between classical bits and qubits

This contrast underscores why qubits offer capabilities far beyond classical bits. Superposition enables *quantum parallelism*, where a qubit encodes multiple possibilities simultaneously, potentially allowing quantum computers to process an exponential number of states with relatively few physical resources. Furthermore, entanglement—a uniquely quantum correlation between qubits—provides intriguing forms of coordination impossible in classical systems, laying the groundwork for quantum teleportation, secure communication, and novel computational algorithms.

Practically, these features translate into advantages in specific computational and information-theoretic tasks. Quantum algorithms, such as Shor's factoring algorithm, exploit coherent superpositions and entanglement to solve certain problems exponentially faster than any known classical algorithm. Quantum cryptography leverages these principles to guarantee security based on the fundamental laws of physics, rather than assumptions about computational hardness. Yet, this potential remains contingent on the challenges of maintaining coherence and controlling quantum states precisely, exemplifying the delicate trade-offs involved.

In sum, qubits generalize classical bits by inhabiting a richer and more nuanced state space, where information is encoded not just as binary digits but as complex quantum waves of probability amplitudes. This quantum leap offers revolutionary possibilities, transforming computing from a simple binary counting game into an exploration of nature's intrinsic probabilistic and interconnected fabric. Understanding this leap is key to appreciating why quantum computing holds the promise to unlock new realms of information processing and secure communication.

1.3 Superposition and Probability

One of the most striking features of quantum mechanics is the principle of *superposition*, which lies at the heart of how quantum states combine and eventually produce observable outcomes. Unlike classical systems that inhabit a definite state at any moment—say, a coin landed heads or tails—a quantum system can simultaneously exist in multiple states until measured. This principle challenges our everyday intuition, revealing a richer, more nuanced tapestry underlying physical reality.

Formally, superposition means that a quantum state can be expressed as a linear combination of a chosen set of basis states. Imagine a set of fundamental quantum states—denoted as $|i\rangle$—that serve as a reference framework, much like the coordinate axes in geometry. Then, any quantum state $|\psi\rangle$ can be written as

$$|\psi\rangle = \sum_i \alpha_i |i\rangle,$$

9

where the coefficients α_i are complex numbers known as *probability amplitudes*. These amplitudes tell a story far richer than classical probabilities. Not only do their magnitudes influence the likelihood of observing a particular outcome, but their complex phases encode subtle interference effects that are fundamentally responsible for quintessentially quantum phenomena.

These probability amplitudes are best thought of as quantum counterparts to classical probabilities, but with the twist of complex values. The squared magnitude of an amplitude, $|\alpha_i|^2$, gives the probability of detecting the system in the corresponding basis state $|i\rangle$. In essence, while the α_i themselves can be positive, negative, or even imaginary numbers, the measured outcomes are always probabilities between zero and one, ensuring the consistency of the theory. The translation from amplitude to probability is given succinctly by the Born rule:

$$P(i) = |\alpha_i|^2.$$

This deceptively simple formula, proposed by Max Born in the 1920s, elegantly connects the mathematical formalism of quantum states to experimentally observable frequencies. Born's insight transformed the abstract wavefunction into a predictive tool bridging theory and measurement.

The complex nature of α_i introduces something entirely new to physics: the relative *phase* between amplitudes. These phase factors are not mere mathematical curiosities but have profound physical consequences. When multiple amplitudes combine, their phases determine whether they add up constructively, amplifying the probability of an outcome, or destructively, canceling each other out and suppressing certain results altogether. This phenomenon is known as *quantum interference*.

To visualize interference, consider the classic double-slit experiment with electrons or photons. Each particle passes through two slits simultaneously—thanks to superposition—and the probability amplitudes for each path combine at a detection screen. Where the waves corresponding to the two paths align in phase, bright fringes appear, marking regions of high probability. Conversely, where they are out of phase, dark fringes form, revealing areas with almost no chance of detection. Such interference patterns are direct evidence that quantum states do not merely coexist side by side; they interact in a wave-like manner, painting a picture of reality richer than classical intuition allows.

Experiments with photons and electrons repeatedly confirm these interference fringes, elegantly demonstrating that quantum superposition is no abstract fancy but a measurable physical fact. For instance, single-photon interference experiments show that even individual particles, sent one at a time, generate an interference pattern over many trials. This reveals the fundamental probabilistic and wave-like nature of quantum entities, bridging the particle-wave duality long debated in physics.

Beyond foundational curiosities, superposition has profound practical implications, especially in the rapidly evolving field of quantum computing. The power of superposition allows quantum bits, or qubits, to inhabit a multitude of states simultaneously rather than being confined to classical zeros or ones. This capability enables quantum algorithms to process an exponential number of possibilities in parallel, achieving computational feats unattainable with classical machines. For example, Grover's search algorithm leverages amplitude amplification, an interference-driven process, to search unsorted databases quadratically faster than any classical

11

counterpart.

The story of superposition extends naturally to systems with multiple components through the concept of *entanglement*. When two or more qubits become entangled, their combined state cannot be factored into separate superpositions for each qubit; instead, they share a joint superposition with correlations stronger than classical physics permits. Entanglement enriches the landscape of quantum information, transforming the simple superposition of a single qubit into a web of intertwined probabilities and phases that enable phenomena like quantum teleportation and superdense coding.

Through this lens, superposition transcends its initial role as a mathematical construction, becoming the gateway to distinctly quantum realities where possibilities coexist and interfere, probabilities quantify fundamental uncertainty, and rich correlations redefine how information can be processed and communicated. By understanding these principles and their experimental confirmations, we glimpse the profound ways quantum mechanics reshapes our grasp of nature, from the smallest particles to the algorithms of the future.

1.4 Entanglement Explained

Quantum theory challenges our classical intuitions not just through uncertainty or superposition, but most strikingly via *entanglement*—a phenomenon where particles become so deeply connected that the state of one cannot be fully described without reference to the other, regardless of distance. To grasp how entanglement underpins quantum networking, it helps to revisit the mathematics and conceptual leaps that distinguish it from everyday correlations.

When dealing with multiple quantum particles, such as qubits in a quantum network, their combined state is described by the *tensor product* of individual states. If one particle is in state $|\psi\rangle$ and another in state $|\phi\rangle$, the joint state is written as $|\psi\rangle \otimes |\phi\rangle$. This product state fully characterizes the composite system, if the particles are independent or only classically correlated. Such composite states are termed *separable* or *product* states—they embody the idea that knowledge about the entire system comes straightforwardly from its parts.

However, quantum mechanics allows for states that cannot be written as simple tensor products. These are *entangled states*, where the whole is more than the sum of its parts. To illustrate, consider the canonical Bell state:

$$|\Phi^+\rangle = \frac{|00\rangle + |11\rangle}{\sqrt{2}}.$$

Here, neither qubit individually occupies a well-defined state; instead, their joint state is a superposition of both being $|0\rangle$ and both being $|1\rangle$. This inseparability is the hallmark of entanglement. If we attempt to describe either qubit alone, tracing out the other, the result is a maximally mixed state, revealing complete uncertainty—yet when measured jointly, their outcomes display perfect correlation.

These correlations are *nonclassical*. Classical physics and intuition suggest that any correlations must be explained by shared history or hidden variables established before measurement. Yet entangled pairs defy this reasoning. The statistical correlations observed violate constraints known as Bell inequalities, which formalize the limits imposed by *local realism*—the idea that physical properties exist prior to and independent of observation, and

13

no influence can travel faster than light.

A famous formulation is the Clauser-Horne-Shimony-Holt (CHSH) inequality, expressed as:

$$|\langle A_1 B_1 \rangle + \langle A_1 B_2 \rangle + \langle A_2 B_1 \rangle - \langle A_2 B_2 \rangle| \leq 2,$$

where A_i and B_j represent measurement outcomes for two distant observers choosing between different measurement settings. Quantum entanglement permits correlations that exceed this bound, reaching up to $2\sqrt{2}$, a clear demonstration of quantum nonlocality where measurement outcomes appear instantaneously intertwined beyond classical explanation.

This baffling feature was at the heart of the Einstein-Podolsky-Rosen (EPR) paradox posed in 1935. Einstein and colleagues argued that quantum mechanics must be incomplete; entanglement seemed to allow "spooky action at a distance," violating locality, or else quantum states could not provide a full description of reality. Yet subsequent experimental tests, beginning with Alain Aspect's landmark experiments in the 1980s and continuing with ever more refined setups, have consistently verified the predictions of quantum mechanics. These *experimental violations* of Bell inequalities leave little room for hidden variable theories compatible with locality, firmly establishing entanglement as a genuine physical resource.

Beyond its conceptual intrigue, entanglement forms the engine that powers a variety of quantum communication protocols promising capabilities far beyond classical limits. For instance, *quantum teleportation* employs entangled pairs to transmit an unknown quantum state from one location to another without moving the physical particle itself—an achievement impossible in classical physics. Similarly, *superdense coding* leverages entanglement to send two classical bits of information by transmitting a single qubit, doubling communication capacity. Perhaps most famously, *quantum key distribution* (QKD) exploits entanglement's inherent security to establish encryption keys immune to eavesdropping, a cornerstone of quantum cryptography.

Building scalable quantum networks, however, encounters practical challenges, mainly because entanglement is fragile and typically established over short distances. This is where the ingenious concept of *entanglement swapping* becomes crucial. By performing special joint measurements on pairs of entangled qubits situated at intermediate nodes, one can generate entanglement between distant, noninteracting qubits—effectively *swapping* entanglement from local pairs to long-range connections. This procedure forms the backbone of *quantum repeaters*, indispensable for extending entanglement across a quantum internet.

Altogether, the study of entanglement reshapes how we understand correlation itself. It reveals nature's capacity for connectedness that defies classical causality and locality, yet remains fully consistent within quantum theory. In quantum networks, entanglement is not just a theoretical curiosity but a powerful resource enabling secure communication, distributed quantum computation, and fundamentally new technologies. The richness and subtlety of entangled states offer a glimpse into a deeper quantum fabric, inviting us to rethink the boundaries of communication and information in the most profound ways.

1.5 Measurement and the Observer Effect

At the heart of quantum mechanics lies a surprising and profoundly unsettling truth: the act of observation itself irreversibly alters the state of the quantum system being observed. This phenomenon, often called the *observer effect*, is not simply a practical limitation or a matter of imperfect instruments; it emerges from the very principles governing the microscopic world. Unlike classical physics, where measurement can be imagined as a passive process, quantum measurement actively changes the system in a fundamental way.

The *Measurement Postulate* encapsulates this formally. It states that when we measure a quantum system, described by some state ρ, the outcome corresponds to one of the possible measurement results, each associated with a mathematical object called a *projection operator* P_i. Crucially, the state *collapses*—that is, it instantaneously jumps—from its original superposition to a new state consistent with the measurement outcome observed. In other words, before measurement, the system might simultaneously hold multiple potential states, but after measurement, only the state corresponding to the observed value remains.

This state-update rule is expressed elegantly through *projection formalism*:

$$\rho \to \frac{P_i\,\rho\,P_i}{\mathrm{Tr}(P_i\,\rho)}$$

Here, ρ represents the initial quantum state (often a density matrix for mixed or pure states), P_i is the projection operator corresponding to the measurement outcome i, and $\mathrm{Tr}(\cdot)$ denotes the trace, ensuring proper normalization. The system's state after measurement is projected onto the subspace associated with P_i and then normalized—the denominator guaranteeing the post-measurement state has total probability one.

This mathematical step translates physically to what is known as *wavefunction collapse*. Unlike the smooth, deterministic evolution prescribed by Schrödinger's equation, the collapse is abrupt and probabilistic. It resigns the system from a potentially rich, multi-faceted superposition into a single reality—the one compatible with the observer's measurement. The collapse, although still debated philosophically, serves as a practical rule explaining why, for example, electrons do not show up in multiple places simultaneously when we look for them, but appear at a definite point.

A subtle but essential concept tied to measurement is *basis dependence*. Quantum states are superpositions relative to a particular choice of basis—essentially, the set of "questions" you ask about the system. For instance, measuring the spin of an electron along the vertical axis projects the system onto "up" or "down" spin states along that axis. However, if instead you choose to measure along a horizontal axis, the possible outcomes and the post-measurement states look entirely different. Thus, the measurement not only collapses the wavefunction but does so in a basis determined by the experimental setup or the specific "observable" being probed. The choice of basis dictates what we can know and what potential realities might emerge.

This interplay between measurement and knowledge leads seamlessly into the *Uncertainty Principle*, perhaps the most famous quantitative expression of the limits imposed by quantum mechanics. It tells us that certain pairs of properties, such as position (x) and momentum (p), cannot both be known with arbitrary precision

17

simultaneously. Sharpening one's knowledge about where a particle is inevitably blurs the knowledge of how fast and in what direction it is moving, and vice versa. This is not a flaw of instruments but a built-in feature of reality itself.

Mathematically, this constraint is expressed as

$$\Delta x \, \Delta p \geq \frac{\hbar}{2}$$

where Δx and Δp represent the uncertainties (standard deviations) in position and momentum, and $\hbar$ is the reduced Planck constant, the fundamental scale of quantum action. The inequality quantifies the intrinsic trade-off in knowledge: the product of uncertainties can never dip below this fundamental limit, emphasizing that some information about a quantum system is inevitably out of reach once measurement is performed.

The physical essence of this uncertainty stems directly from the observer effect: the very act of attempting to measure one variable disturbs conjugate variables. This disturbance is not merely technological; it is a fundamental consequence of quantum evolution interwoven with measurement.

But how exactly does the observer's action influence the system? When we measure a quantum state, we interact with it—sometimes with photons, electrons, or specialized measurement devices. These interactions introduce changes that propagate into the system's future behavior. Unlike classical observation, quantum measurement typically involves entangling the system with the measuring apparatus, forming correlations that enforce the observed outcome while destroying superpositions. This means the quantum state is no longer separable into independent parts; the measurement effectively "locks in" a particular reality.

In the burgeoning field of quantum computation and information, this measurement-induced disturbance manifests vividly. Consider a *qubit*—the quantum analogue of a classical bit. Unlike a bit restricted to 0 or 1, a qubit can exist in any superposition of these states. Reading out its value, known as *qubit readout*, is a delicate operation that must balance fidelity with minimal disturbance. Typical practical methods involve coupling the qubit to resonant cavities or employing fluorescence detection, where measurement outcomes are inferred from indirect signals. These techniques harness the projection postulate but also face the unavoidable consequence: the qubit's state is irrevocably altered during readout, collapsing to a definite 0 or 1 and losing prior quantum coherence.

This leads naturally to the phenomenon of *decoherence*, a subtle but crucial factor in understanding quantum measurement and the observer effect. Decoherence describes how quantum superpositions deteriorate when a system interacts with its environment, even unintentionally. The surrounding environment acts like an incessant "observer," constantly entangling with the system's degrees of freedom and effectively measuring them, thereby destroying delicate interference patterns and turning pure quantum states into statistical mixtures. This loss of coherence blurs the line between pure quantum behavior and the classical world we experience.

Decoherence is both a curse and a guiding principle. It explains why macroscopic objects do not appear as superpositions of different states—they rapidly decohere in everyday conditions—and also guides experimental efforts to isolate quantum systems to preserve coherence for as long as possible, a necessary step for quantum technologies.

Taken together, measurement, wavefunction collapse, basis dependence, and decoherence sketch a profound picture: quantum systems do not merely passively reveal properties upon inspection but are fundamentally transformed by the observer's action. This reshapes our notions of reality and knowledge, showing that the limits of what can be known are not only technical but woven deeply into nature's fabric. In quantum information science, embracing these effects rather than circumventing them allows us to harness new forms of computing, secure communication, and sensing—all resting on a foundation where observation is both a window and a hammer shaping the world beneath.

1.6   The Double-Slit Experiment

The intriguing simplicity of the double-slit experiment conceals profound insights about the quantum world. Originally formulated by Thomas Young in the early 19th century to demonstrate the wave nature of light, the experiment gained renewed significance with the rise of quantum mechanics, where it became a cornerstone for understanding the peculiar behavior of particles at the smallest scales.

At its core, the experimental setup is elegantly straightforward. A source emits particles—whether photons, electrons, or other quantum objects—toward a barrier pierced by two narrow slits placed close together. Beyond the slits lies a detection screen capable of recording individual impacts, creating a visible pattern over time.

Classical intuition offers two clean predictions. If particles behaved like tiny solid bullets, each would pass through one slit or the other, arriving at the screen to produce two bright bands aligned with the openings. No surprises, just like tossing marbles through cracks. By contrast, if waves were involved, the familiar phenomenon of interference would emerge: overlapping ripples from the two slits combine, producing a series of bright and dark fringes on the detection screen—regions of constructive and destructive interference respectively.

Quantum mechanics, however, refuses to settle for this dichotomy. When particles such as electrons are sent through the apparatus, they do not behave strictly as waves nor purely as particles. Instead, each particle enters a quantum superposition, a state mathematically described as a combination of passing through slit one *and* slit two simultaneously. This isn't a matter of incomplete knowledge; it reflects a fundamental property that the particle's behavior cannot be pinned down until measured.

Mathematically, the wavefunctions associated with each slit, denoted $\psi_1(x)$ and $\psi_2(x)$, add together to yield the total wavefunction at position x on the screen. The probability of detecting the particle at x is given by the intensity

$$I(x) \propto |\psi_1(x) + \psi_2(x)|^2 ,$$

where the squared magnitude accounts for interference effects. Peaks and troughs appear as a result of this coherent sum: where waves reinforce one another, detection is more likely; where they cancel out, it is suppressed.

This conceptual leap gains striking experimental support when particles are fired one at a time. Even as individual impacts accumulate seemingly at random, a

pattern of bright and dark fringes gradually emerges—
an interference pattern born from single-particle
wavefunctions interfering with themselves. Such a
phenomenon defies classical explanation, since no
multi-particle collaboration is possible; each particle,
isolated and independent, exhibits wave-like self-
interference.

Intriguingly, the pattern changes if one attempts to determine *which slit* the particle passes through. Any measurement or detector that extracts this "which-path" information collapses the delicate superposition. The interference disappears, reverting the distribution on the
screen to two concentrated clusters aligned with each slit.
The very act of observation alters the outcome.

This puzzling feature has inspired numerous delayed-
choice experiments, where the decision to observe
or not is postponed until after the particle passes
through the slits.   To the surprise of many, such
setups suggest the measurement choice retroactively
influences the particle's prior state—a mind-bending
result that challenges conventional notions of causality
and temporal order.

Beyond its enigmatic implications, the double-slit experiment crystallizes several foundational lessons in quantum theory. It vividly illustrates *complementarity*: the
mutual exclusivity of particle-like and wave-like descriptions depending on measurement context. It forces us to
question classical realism—that physical properties exist
in definite states independent of observation—and emphasizes the active role of the observer in shaping reality
at the quantum level.

With advances in experimental techniques, the double-
slit concept has been extended well beyond photons and
electrons. Neutrons, atoms, and even large molecules,

such as buckyballs composed of 60 carbon atoms, have been successfully sent through double slits, revealing interference patterns that testify to quantum coherence at unexpected scales. These instances reinforce that the quantum world transcends the microscopic, blurring boundaries between quantum and classical realms.

Together, these variations underscore the universality and robustness of quantum superposition and interference, challenging us to rethink the classic distinctions between waves and particles, matter and information.

The double-slit experiment thrives not only as a hallmark demonstration of quantum strangeness but as a practical gateway to modern technologies. Its core principles underpin emerging quantum networks, where superposition and interference of photons allow secure communication and entanglement distribution over long distances.

By bridging intuitive imagery with a rigorous mathematical framework, the double-slit experiment remains an indispensable guidepost on the journey to unravel the quantum enigma. It encapsulates how the intangible quantum wavefunction shapes the probabilistic reality we ultimately observe, reminding us that measurement, context, and information are inseparable facets of the fabric of nature.

Chapter 2

From Classical to Quantum Communication

This chapter bridges the familiar principles of today's Internet with the emerging paradigms of quantum communication. We begin by reviewing classical network architecture, protocols, and performance considerations. Next, we examine the fundamental limitations of classical systems in security, scalability, and reliability. Building on that foundation, we introduce the unique properties of quantum communication that address these gaps, survey pioneering experiments that proved its feasibility, and explore early hybrid implementations that integrate quantum channels into existing networks. The chapter concludes with a direct comparison between classical and quantum internets, setting the stage for deeper protocol and hardware discussions.

2.1 How the Internet Works Today

Beneath the digital sheen of countless web pages, streaming videos, and instant messages lies a carefully orchestrated dance of protocols, signals, and routers that make the modern Internet hum along seamlessly. To understand how the Internet works today, we

return to its classical foundation—a layered network
architecture built on the venerable TCP/IP model—
through which information journeys from one device to
another across a dizzying tangle of physical media and
logical pathways.

At the heart of this architecture is the concept of *network
layering*, where distinct responsibilities are parceled out
across several conceptual strata. The four primary layers of the TCP/IP stack—link, internet, transport, and
application—form a modular blueprint enabling interoperability and scalability. Starting from the bottom, the
link layer deals with actual data transfer over a physical medium; the internet layer handles logical addressing and routing; the transport layer ensures end-to-end
communication; and the application layer hosts familiar
protocols that users directly interact with.

Delving into the *physical media* that constitutes the
Internet's nervous system, the diversity is striking.
Copper cables, once the backbone of telephony, still
deliver electrical signals over twisted pairs or coaxial
lines, prized for their ubiquity and cost-effectiveness.
Fiber-optics, on the other hand, employ pulses of light
traveling through glass strands, offering dramatically
higher bandwidth and immunity to electromagnetic
interference, thus forming the arteries of high-
capacity backbones and data centers. Finally, wireless
transmission—ranging from Wi-Fi and cellular networks
to satellite links—lends mobility and flexibility, albeit
with challenges such as interference, fading, and limited
range. Together, these media provide the physical
foundation over which digital information is sent and
received.

Before data can traverse thousands of miles, it must be
suitably prepared for the journey through a process
known as *packet switching*. Instead of sending data

26

as a continuous stream, information is broken down into manageable chunks called packets. Each packet carries part of the message, along with addressing and control information, allowing them to travel independently across the network and be reassembled at the destination. This method optimizes bandwidth usage and improves resilience, as packets can be rerouted around congested nodes or broken links, akin to cars taking alternate routes in a busy city.

On the link layer, a critical role is played by *data link functions*, which include mechanisms such as framing, addressing, and error detection. Every device on a local network has a unique physical identifier called a MAC (Media Access Control) address, ensuring packets arrive precisely where intended within that local segment. Frames—formatted data units—encapsulate packets with headers and trailers to delineate boundaries and provide error-checking via simple checksum algorithms. These safeguards detect, and sometimes correct, transmission errors arising from noise or signal degradation, preserving data integrity over the often-unpredictable physical medium.

Moving up a layer, the *internet layer* provides a global addressing system through IP (Internet Protocol) addresses, which function much like postal codes guiding packets toward their destination networks. Assignment of these addresses is governed by hierarchies and allocation policies to ensure uniqueness and efficient routing. Routing itself relies on tables maintained by routers, which dictate the best paths for forwarding packets. These tables are dynamic, constantly updated by routing protocols to adapt to network changes, thereby optimizing the journey of each packet in real time.

Two principal *routing protocols* underpin this dynamic

27

decision-making. Within an organization or a contiguous network domain, the Open Shortest Path First (OSPF) protocol enables routers to share topology information and compute the shortest, most efficient routes collaboratively. For routing between distinct administrative domains—such as between Internet service providers—the Border Gateway Protocol (BGP) governs the exchange of reachability information, facilitating the complex choreography that keeps the global Internet interconnected. BGP's decisions are based not only on shortest path but also on policies and agreements, reflecting economic and political realities layered atop technical ones.

Once packets arrive at their destination network, the *transport layer* steps into the spotlight, orchestrating end-to-end communication between applications. Here, two main protocols prevail: TCP (Transmission Control Protocol) and UDP (User Datagram Protocol). TCP emphasizes reliable delivery, establishing connections, sequencing packets, acknowledging receipt, and retransmitting lost segments—making it the workhorse of web browsing, email, and file transfers. Conversely, UDP offers a lightweight, connectionless service with minimal overhead, sacrificing reliability for speed and low latency; this makes it suited to applications like video streaming, real-time gaming, or Voice over IP, where occasional packet loss is preferable to delay.

The topmost *application layer* is where users experience the Internet's magic through familiar protocols. HTTP (Hypertext Transfer Protocol) powers the World Wide Web, fetching and rendering web pages by requesting resources from servers. The Domain Name System (DNS) quietly translates human-friendly domain names into numerical IP addresses, acting as the Internet's phonebook. For email, SMTP (Simple Mail

Transfer Protocol) moves messages between servers, while POP and IMAP allow retrieval by clients. These protocols, among dozens others, enable a vast ecosystem of services that shape daily life on the Internet.

Underlying these layers is the guiding philosophy known as the *end-to-end principle*, which argues that intelligence and complexity belong primarily at the network edges—in endpoints such as computers and smartphones—rather than in the core infrastructure. By keeping the network simple and agnostic about data content, the Internet achieves remarkable flexibility and extensibility, allowing novel applications and services to flourish without requiring fundamental network redesign. This principle explains why the Internet, despite its age, continues to evolve and scale gracefully.

With growing demands on bandwidth and diverse types of data traffic, *Quality of Service* (QoS) management has become essential to maintain smooth performance. Techniques such as traffic prioritization, shaping, and resource reservation ensure that latency-sensitive applications like voice calls or video conferences receive timely delivery, while less time-critical data like file downloads wait their turn. Routers and switches apply these policies dynamically, balancing competing flows so that users experience consistent, predictable behavior even during peak usage.

Together, these elements form the classical core of today's Internet: a distributed, adaptive system where packets traverse heterogeneous media guided by layered protocols, complex routing algorithms, and evolving management strategies. This design provides the robust, flexible foundation upon which innovations continue to be built, from the simplest email to the most advanced streaming services, quietly enabling the digital world as we know it.

2.2 Limitations of Classical Networks

Classical networks—the sprawling global web of interconnected devices forming today's Internet—have transformed how we communicate, work, and play. Yet beneath their apparent robustness lies a tangle of challenges that continue to curb their performance, security, and scalability. Understanding these constraints is crucial not only for appreciating current technological limits but also for recognizing the impetus behind emerging paradigms in networking.

- **Scalability Challenges**

  At first glance, the Internet seems infinitely expandable, effortlessly connecting billions of devices. However, the physical and topological infrastructure imposes hard limits. Copper wires and fiber optic cables, while capable, face diminishing returns with each additional node. Network topologies—often hierarchical or star-based—hit bottlenecks as new devices add traffic bursts and routing complexity. Expanding capacity isn't just a matter of adding hardware; the underlying protocols must grapple with managing vastly increased routing tables and maintaining efficiency without overburdening resources.

  Moreover, wireless networks confront spatial constraints like signal attenuation and interference, which limit the density of devices within a given area. The more users crammed into the airwaves, the more they compete for a finite spectrum, resulting in degraded performance. This phenomenon is not exclusive to wireless; in both wired and wireless realms, scaling brings diminishing returns, forcing network architects to devise intricate load balancing and hierarchical subnetting that, while clever, add layers of complexity and potential points of failure.

- **Bandwidth Bottlenecks**

  Within these scaling constraints lie the often frustrating realities of bandwidth limitations. Classical networks typically rely on shared media—be it cable segments, radio frequencies, or switches—that distribute available throughput among multiple users. During peak demand, this shared nature manifests starkly: streaming videos freeze, large downloads slow, and video calls stutter.

  The crux is that bandwidth is a finite resource. When multiple applications or users simultaneously demand high throughput, contention creates a bottleneck. These peak-load scenarios reveal a fundamental limitation—the inability of network resources to elastically expand in real time. While technological advances have pushed raw bandwidth upward, the last-mile connections, congested routers, and backbone links can still become choke points. The experience is all too familiar: no matter how fast your own connection is, the slowest link on your communication path dominates your effective speed.

- **Latency and Jitter**

  Beyond raw bandwidth, delay matters a great deal. Latency—the time taken for data to traverse the network—can make the difference between a smooth video call and an awkward stammer. Even more disruptive is jitter, the variability in delay from packet to packet. For real-time applications such as online gaming, voice-over-IP, or telemedicine, these issues are not mere

31

annoyances but critical obstacles.

Classical networks were initially designed with robustness and throughput in mind rather than minimizing delay. Packets follow different routes, experience queuing delays in routers, and occasionally require retransmission due to errors. This unpredictability sows jitter, which forces applications to buffer data, introducing further delay. The layered architecture, while versatile, often handles this problem at higher protocol levels, adding complexity and overhead. In scenarios demanding immediate feedback or synchronization, these inherent timing fluctuations limit user experience and application viability.

- **Security Vulnerabilities**

  Security in classical networks remains an ongoing battle. The fundamental design principles of openness and interoperability introduce vulnerabilities: data traverses numerous intermediaries, each a potential point of attack. Eavesdropping, where malicious actors silently listen to communication, is alarmingly straightforward on many networks. Worse still, man-in-the-middle (MitM) attacks enable adversaries to intercept, alter, or forge messages without detection.

  Classical networks must therefore rely heavily on cryptographic safeguards, layered protocols, and vigilant monitoring to preserve confidentiality and integrity. Yet this arms race between defenders and attackers continues unabated. The problem is compounded by the assumption that endpoints and infrastructure are often untrusted, requiring a complex web of trust relationships and security protocols that can be difficult to manage and audit. As the number of connected devices skyrockets, so too does the attack surface.

- **Cryptographic Dependence**

  The security architecture of today's networks rests primarily on computational hardness assumptions. Encryption algorithms such as RSA or AES rely on mathematical problems that are difficult to solve with current computing resources. While effective now, this cryptographic dependence is inherently fragile: advances in computing power—particularly the potential arrival of quantum computers—threaten to undermine these foundations.

  Unlike a physical law offering absolute security, cryptographic schemes offer conditional security, reliant on keeping certain problems practically unsolvable for adversaries. This temporal fragility forces a continuous cycle of upgrading standards and protocols. The result is a perpetual race to stay ahead, often demanding significant resources for cryptanalysis, updates, and audits. Hence, classical networks' security is as strong as the weakest link in both technology and human management.

- **Key Distribution Problems**

  A notorious Achilles' heel in securing communications is key distribution. Whether symmetric (shared secret keys) or asymmetric (public-private key pairs), securely sharing and managing these keys at scale is remarkably difficult. Improper key management can nullify

the strongest cryptographic algorithms, leaving
data exposed.

In large networks, the overhead of distributing
and revoking keys grows exponentially with
the number of users and devices. Public Key
Infrastructure (PKI), certificate authorities,
and federated trust models attempt to address
this, but they introduce complexity, potential
bottlenecks, and points of centralization. Devices
must trust these intermediaries, and failures
or compromises can cascade widely. This
undercurrent problem quietly undermines the
promise of secure communication in classical
networks.

- **Single Points of Failure**

  Despite the Internet's reputation as a decentralized
  system, many classical networks host critical
  centralized services that become single points
  of failure. Domain Name Servers (DNS),
  authentication servers, cloud service providers—
  all act as pivotal hubs. When these fail or are
  attacked, the ripple effects can be massive: entire
  websites become unreachable, authentication
  services halt, and data centers suffer outages.

  These bottlenecks not only impact performance but
  also security. Centralized control points are entic-
  ing targets for attackers and surveillance. Moreover, geographic and organizational concentration
  can limit resilience to natural disasters, political interference, or hardware failures. Attempts at redundancy and distribution mitigate these risks but
  can never fully eliminate the fundamental trade-off
  between manageability and decentralization.

- **Error-Handling Overhead**

Unlike physical infrastructure designed to prevent failures, classical networks embrace error and loss as inevitable realities. Various layers of protocols detect and correct errors—through retransmissions, acknowledgments, and checksums—incurring overhead. While essential for reliable communication, this error-handling is costly in terms of bandwidth, latency, and complexity.

For instance, a lost packet in a TCP stream triggers retransmission, potentially doubling the data sent for that segment and adding delay. Higher-level protocols must also manage congestion control, retransmissions, and synchronization, further taxing network resources. This layered error control, though elegant, reflects a compromise between performance and reliability that classical networks must constantly juggle.

- **Regulatory and Jurisdictional Issues**

  The physical infrastructure of the Internet spans national borders, yet legal and regulatory regimes remain fragmented. Governments impose diverse laws governing data privacy, encryption, censorship, and cross-border data flows. These conflicting frameworks create barriers to seamless global communication and complicate the deployment of uniform security standards.

  For businesses and users, regulatory uncertainty can delay innovation or force fragmented implementations that undercut interoperability. Encryption standards, for example, vary widely, with some countries restricting key lengths or mandating backdoors. The resulting landscape is a mosaic of legal and technical constraints

35

reflecting geopolitical realities, which classical
networks must navigate without compromising
their fundamental nature or user trust.

The classical network architecture is a marvel of ingenuity and adaptation. Yet its intrinsic limitations—scaling
bottlenecks, bandwidth constraints, unpredictable
latency, security vulnerabilities dependent on fragile
cryptographic assumptions, key distribution dilemmas,
centralized chokepoints, error-correction overhead, and
a maze of regulatory entanglements—paint a picture
of a system operating at the edges of its foundational
assumptions.

These limitations not only shape current user
experiences but also drive the relentless quest for
new paradigms: from software-defined and quantum
networks to decentralized architectures and post-
quantum cryptography. Grappling with the classical
Internet's shortcomings reveals the ongoing dance
between innovation and inevitability in the ever-
evolving story of connectivity.

2.3 A Need for Quantum Communica-
tion

In a world increasingly shaped by digital connections,
the way we share information has become a cornerstone
of modern life—powering everything from financial
transactions to private conversations and government
communications. Yet classical communication
systems, built upon decades-old internet protocols
and encryption methods, face fundamental and
practical constraints that limit their security and
efficiency. Quantum communication emerges not as
an incremental improvement, but as a decisive solution

addressing these inherent limitations. To understand why quantum approaches have captured such interest, it is essential to examine both the vulnerabilities of classical methods and the unique strengths brought by quantum laws.

Central to the motivation for quantum communication is the quest for *unconditional security*. Traditional cryptographic schemes often rely on mathematical problems presumed to be hard, such as factoring large numbers or the discrete logarithm problem. While these assumptions have held up well so far, advances in computing—including the looming threat of quantum computers—could undermine these foundations overnight. Quantum communication sidesteps this uncertainty by grounding security in the immutable principles of quantum mechanics. Unlike classical encryption, whose strength hinges on computational difficulty, quantum security is fundamentally guaranteed by the laws of nature themselves. This means no amount of computational power—even a hypothetical quantum computer—can break the security provided by quantum protocols.

A hallmarked feature of quantum security is its ability to detect eavesdropping directly. Classical messages, encoded as bits travelling through wires or waves, can be intercepted, copied, and resent without leaving a trace. Quantum communication breaks this mold: information is carried in quantum states of particles, such as photons, whose delicate nature is easily disturbed by measurement. Any attempt at interception inevitably alters these quantum states, betraying the presence of an eavesdropper. This intrinsic property enables communicating parties to verify the integrity of their channel before exchanging any secret information, offering a level of trust unattainable in classical settings.

The fundamental reason behind this fragility of quantum information is encapsulated in the *no-cloning theorem*, a pivotal result in quantum mechanics that forbids the creation of identical copies of an unknown quantum state. More formally, there exists no unitary operator U such that for an unknown state $|\psi\rangle$ and a blank state $|0\rangle$, the relation

$$U|\psi\rangle|0\rangle = |\psi\rangle|\psi\rangle$$

holds true for all $|\psi\rangle$. This principle immediately halts any eavesdropper's hope of replicating quantum data stealthily. Unlike classical signals, which can be perfectly copied and redistributed at will, quantum states demand a subtler and more delicate handling. This restriction not only safeguards the data but also reshapes the very strategies for communication and security.

Building on these principles, one of the flagship quantum communication protocols is *Quantum Key Distribution* (QKD). This method enables two parties to generate shared, secret cryptographic keys with provable security guaranteed by the physics underlying quantum systems. Instead of transmitting messages through noisy classical channels and hoping their cryptographic shields hold, QKD transmits the key material itself through a quantum channel, wherein any intruder's interference is detected immediately. Once the key is securely established, classical messages can be encrypted and sent with confidence, knowing that the encryption keys are secret and uncorrupted.

Quantum communication, however, is not solely about secrecy. Perhaps more striking is its radical approach to information transfer embodied in the concept of *quantum teleportation*. Contrary to the popular sci-fi notion of beaming humans across space, quantum teleportation transmits an unknown quantum state from one location to another, using a combination of entanglement—a deeply mysterious quantum correlation shared between particles—and classical communication. The original state is destroyed in the process to ensure that the no-cloning theorem is upheld, but the receiver reconstructs an exact copy. This protocol demonstrates quantum communication's power to move delicate quantum information across distances, opening avenues for distributed quantum computing and fundamentally new communication paradigms.

At the heart of many quantum communication protocols lies *entanglement as a resource*. Entangled particles share a connection so profound that the measurement of one instantaneously influences the state of the other, regardless of the distance between them. This phenomenon—once dismissed as "spooky action at a distance" by Einstein—has become a practical tool for secure communication and error correction. By leveraging entanglement, parties can establish correlations impossible to simulate classically, creating channels that are simultaneously robust and insightful about their security. Such nonlocal correlations provide not only a new layer of security but also novel capabilities like device-independent cryptography, where users need not trust the hardware itself as long as certain measurement statistics are observed.

Despite its promise, quantum communication faces a significant hurdle: the *integration imperative*. The vast existing communication infrastructure—fibre optics, satellites, wireless networks—is overwhelmingly classical, engineered for decades around classical signals and protocols. Overlaying quantum channels on this infrastructure is a challenging and ongoing endeavor. Quantum signals are exquisitely sensitive and cannot be amplified without introducing noise,

a luxury that classical signals enjoy. Bridging these
worlds requires innovative engineering solutions such
as quantum repeaters and entanglement swapping
stations to extend quantum links and maintain signal
fidelity over long distances. It also demands rethinking
network architectures and protocols to accommodate
quantum operations alongside classical data traffic.

The potential applications driving research and
investment into quantum communication are diverse
and profound. Secure messaging is the most immediate
and tangible, allowing journalists, diplomats, and
businesses to communicate with absolute confidence
in the secrecy of their exchanges. Beyond secure
messaging lies *distributed quantum computing*, where
quantum processors, separated geographically,
cooperate through entangled quantum links—enabling
computational feats impossible on any single device.
Additionally, networks of entangled sensors promise
enhanced measurement precision for everything from
gravitational wave detection to navigation without GPS,
unlocking novel scientific and technological capabilities.

Navigating from experimental demonstrations to
widespread deployment requires a *roadmap overview*
that envisions a phased transition. Early stages focus
on point-to-point QKD links connecting critical nodes,
such as government agencies or financial centers. As
technology matures, quantum repeaters and satellite-
based quantum communication will enable regional
networks to interlink, forming the backbone of a global
quantum internet. Ultimately, this quantum network
will coexist with classical systems, providing layered
security and novel information transfer functionalities
that classical channels alone cannot match.

The compelling need to move beyond classical
communication is underscored by a convergence

of factors: the impending obsolescence of classical
cryptographic assumptions, the unique ability to detect
and thwart eavesdropping, the fundamental quantum
limits on copying and sharing information, and the
imaginative new protocols enabled by entanglement
and teleportation. These drivers collectively paint a
picture of quantum communication as not just desirable,
but essential—offering a fundamentally new paradigm
that could transform how we think about, protect, and
share information in the 21st century and beyond.

2.4 Pioneering Quantum Communication Experiments

The promise of quantum communication rests on the
extraordinary properties of quantum mechanics—to
transmit information with unparalleled security and
efficiency. However, bold concepts rarely become
reality without rigorous experimentation. Landmark
demonstrations have forged the path from theoretical
blueprints to practical quantum networks, testing and
validating key principles along the way. Examining
these pioneering experiments not only highlights
human ingenuity but also reveals the subtleties faced in
harnessing the quantum world for communication.

The journey began with the implementation of the BB84
protocol[1], the first quantum key distribution scheme
that exploited the peculiarities of single photons to
establish secret keys. The initial BB84 prototype was
realized using fiber-optic cables, marking a fundamental
shift from chalkboard ideas to tangible reality. This
early system managed to transmit quantum bits—or

---

[1]Named after the year 1984 and its inventors Charles Bennett and
Gilles Brassard

qubits—encoded in photon polarizations over short
distances of optical fiber. Though modest by today's
standards, the experiment skillfully balanced photon
sources, detectors, and the fiber's inherent imperfections
to achieve secure key rates sufficient for practical use.
Performance metrics, such as quantum bit error
rates and key generation speeds, established baseline
expectations and illuminated obstacles like photon loss
and detector inefficiencies. This prototype laid the
groundwork for a growing confidence in fiber-based
quantum communications.

Shortly after, the 1991 Ekert protocol introduced a
captivating twist by relying on quantum entanglement
rather than individual photons. In this setup, pairs
of entangled photons are distributed to two distant
parties, and their measurement outcomes—deeply
correlated beyond classical limits—serve as the basis
for secure key exchange. The hallmark of Ekert's
scheme is its reliance on Bell inequalities to verify
the presence of genuine entanglement, offering an
intrinsic guarantee against eavesdropping. Early
experiments reproduced these conditions, successfully
demonstrating key distribution secured by fundamental
quantum nonlocality. This achievement was more than
technical; it was a conceptual validation that nature's
peculiarities could underpin security, not just the laws
of convention and complexity.

Parallel to key distribution, another quantum networking pillar began to emerge: quantum teleportation.
In ingenious laboratory demonstrations, scientists
transferred the quantum state of a particle from one
node to another without physically moving the particle
itself. These delicate experiments enacted quantum
state transfer using entangled photon pairs and
classical communication channels, weaving together

measurements and unitary operations. Although teleportation did not move matter faster than light, it epitomized the ability to transmit quantum information intact, a requirement for scalable quantum networks. The experimental successes served as proof of principle that quantum states could be faithfully transmitted between nodes, crucial for developing quantum repeaters and complex communication infrastructures.

Expanding the reach of quantum communication became the next hurdle. While early experiments operated over tens of kilometers, a series of long-distance fiber trials shattered these confines. By optimizing photon sources, low-loss optical fibers, and sophisticated detectors, researchers achieved record-setting distances exceeding 100 kilometers in real-world fiber networks. These trials tackled photon absorption and dispersion, elevating the feasibility of city-wide quantum communication and beyond. They also underscored the need for quantum repeaters—devices still under development—to extend these distances further without compromising quantum coherence.

Recognizing fiber's geographical limits, researchers turned their sights upward, exploring free-space optical tests. These line-of-sight experiments transmitted quantum keys through the atmosphere, bridging urban rooftops or air-gaps with remarkable precision. Free-space QKD had to combat atmospheric turbulence, background light, and alignment challenges, pushing the bounds of optical engineering. Yet, successful demonstrations across tens of kilometers in city environments validated the potential for flexible, on-demand quantum links in places where fiber installation is impractical. These insights not only complemented fiber-based systems but also envisioned networks spanning satellite-ground links.

Satellites soon became the ultimate proving grounds for quantum communication, where the challenges transcended terrestrial concerns. Orbital quantum key distribution missions, such as those launched in the 2010s, achieved quantum communication between spaceborne platforms and ground stations, overcoming photon loss, Doppler shifts, and precise timing synchronization. These missions established trusted keys over thousands of kilometers and heralded a new era in global-scale quantum networks. By demonstrating that quantum information could survive the rigors of space, satellite QKD became a symbol of technological ambition turning science fiction into science fact.

Back on Earth, metropolitan QKD networks integrated multiple nodes within dense city environments, realizing the first multi-user quantum communication infrastructures. These testbeds coordinated crucial classical and quantum hardware, addressing routing, user authentication, and resource sharing. The deployment in live city networks affirmed the practicality of quantum communication beyond isolated laboratory demonstrations, anticipating near-future applications in securing financial transactions, government communications, and critical infrastructure. Such networks illuminated how quantum communication could weave seamlessly into existing digital ecosystems.

These remarkable achievements were made possible by surmounting formidable engineering challenges. Photon loss, the nemesis of quantum signals, demanded ultra-low-loss fibers, precise alignment of optical components, and improved single-photon detectors with high efficiency and low noise. Synchronization of spatially distributed nodes to femtosecond precision was vital for ensuring temporal overlap of entangled photons and minimizing errors. Environmental noise—from temperature fluctuations to vibrations—required adaptive stabilization techniques and real-time feedback systems. Each obstacle spurred creative solutions that continue to enrich the design of quantum communication hardware and protocols.

The experimental timeline unfolds as a compelling narrative of scientific perseverance. Beginning in the 1980s with theoretical protocols and simple tabletop setups, the 1990s saw early fiber BB84 implementations and entanglement experiments. The turn of the millennium expanded range and robustness through longer fibers and free-space trials. The 2010s marked a leap with satellite missions and metropolitan networks, increasingly integrating quantum communication with classical infrastructure. Each milestone not only confirmed the foundational physics but progressively carved a path toward practical deployment.

Together, these pioneering quantum communication experiments have transformed abstract principles into reproducible technologies, anchoring the fledgling field in empirical success. By validating quantum key distribution protocols, demonstrating entanglement's power to secure communication, enabling quantum state transfer, extending distance records, and tackling real-world engineering obstacles, they established the essential building blocks of quantum networking. These experiments hold the promise of reshaping how information is shared in the coming decades—more secure, more private, and fundamentally quantum.

2.5 Blending Classical and Quantum Systems

Bridging the worlds of classical and quantum networks is no small feat. Today's communication infrastructure, exquisitely honed over decades, must gracefully accommodate the delicate, often elusive nature of quantum signals. The challenge lies not only in physical compatibility but also in conceptual harmony—marrying the robustness and ubiquity of classical networks with the fragile quantum states that promise unprecedented capabilities in security and computation. This blend demands novel architectures, carefully engineered hardware, and sophisticated control mechanisms that together compose a hybrid ecosystem.

Hybrid Network Topologies

Mapping quantum links onto existing networks calls for innovative topological designs that allow classical and quantum traffic to coexist without mutual disruption. Three prevailing models have emerged: overlay, tandem, and integrated.

- The *overlay* model treats the quantum network as a virtual layer atop the classical one, much like how the internet's routing protocols overlay physical cables. Here, quantum channels ride on dedicated fibers or links separate from classical data streams, simplifying isolation but increasing deployment cost.

- The *tandem* approach arranges classical and quantum connections in sequence—classical segments forward routing control and management signals, while quantum segments handle sensitive quantum transmissions. Tandem models are beneficial where quantum repeaters are sparsely interspersed within classical routes, ensuring easier interoperability without simultaneous physical layering.

- The *integrated* model fully combines both traffic types over shared physical infrastructure. This is the most ambitious and resource-efficient scenario, seizing every wavelength and fiber to its utmost potential. But it also demands extreme care to prevent cross-talk or noise contamination, especially as quantum signals are remarkably susceptible to disruption from classical light.

Together, these topological choices reflect a pragmatic balance of performance, cost, and technological readiness, guiding network architects in their quest to meld the two paradigms effectively.

Wavelength Division Multiplexing: Sharing the Same Road

Much like urban traffic uses multiple lanes to ease congestion, modern fiber optic networks employ *Wavelength Division Multiplexing* (WDM) to transmit multiple channels simultaneously at different light frequencies. Leveraging WDM is a natural first step in enabling quantum and classical signals to co-propagate on a single fiber optic strand, reducing infrastructure redundancy and deployment hurdles.

However, mixing these signals is akin to threading a silk thread through a bustling highway: quantum photons, inherently delicate, can fall prey to scattering, Raman noise, and subtle nonlinear effects generated by the powerful classical beams sharing the fiber. Advances in filtering techniques and precise wavelength allocation—particularly assigning quantum channels to less noisy spectral bands—have dramatically improved coexistence viability.

Thus, WDM serves as a cornerstone technology, facilitating a graceful fusion of classical bandwidth abundance with quantum subtlety, an elegant choreography of light.

Quantum/Classical Interfaces

Physical integration hinges upon specialized hardware modules that mediate the transition between quantum and classical realms. These interfaces perform functions analogous to traffic controllers and customs checkpoints—routing photons, buffering quantum states, and converting signals into forms amenable for different hardware or protocol layers.

Quantum-classical routers, for instance, selectively direct single photons based on routing information transmitted classically, without disturbing the quantum information encoded. Quantum memories and buffers play a crucial role in temporarily storing fragile quantum states, enabling synchronization among asynchronous classical control signals and quantum data flows.

Signal converters translate quantum states into classical measurement outcomes or vice versa, indispensable for hybrid devices like quantum key distribution terminals that rely on classical post-processing for error correction and privacy amplification. This hardware symbiosis is essential, as it allows classical subsystems—long reliable and scalable—to shepherd quantum communications safely through the network.

Control and Management Planes

While the physical layer juggles photons and fibers, the network's intelligence rides upon its *control and management planes.* Here, software frameworks orchestrate allocation of resources like bandwidth, channel time, and routing paths across both quantum and classical domains.

Integrating control planes requires harmonizing disparate network management protocols. For example, classical networks utilize proven signaling and routing protocols such as the Border Gateway Protocol (BGP), whereas quantum networks demand highly precise scheduling and entanglement distribution protocols, often unique to hardware capabilities.

Emerging software-defined networking (SDN) concepts are increasingly vital, providing centralized, programmable control that can dynamically adapt routes to optimize quantum key rates or recover from faults, all while maintaining compatibility with classical traffic priorities. The fusion of classical and quantum management thus forms a delicate ballet of coordination, enabling hybrid networks to perform harmoniously.

Synchronization Techniques

Quantum protocols frequently depend on finely tuned timing—imagine coordinating a flawless dance where every step depends on a shared beat. Synchronizing clocks across geographically separated nodes to within picoseconds is a formidable challenge but essential for operations like entanglement swapping and quantum teleportation.

Classical networks already employ sophisticated protocols like IEEE 1588 Precision Time Protocol (PTP), and Global Positioning System (GPS) signals provide coarse alignment. However, quantum networking pushes demands further, requiring improved clock distribution and timing alignment techniques capable of real-time adjustments to quantum channel fluctuations.

Innovative solutions include distributing synchronization photons alongside quantum signals, exploiting
ultrastable optical frequency combs, or employing
quantum-enhanced timing protocols themselves.
Such advances ensure quantum states generated and
measured at different nodes share a precise temporal
frame, vital for reliable quantum communication.

Error Monitoring

While classical networks rely on standardized error
detection and correction techniques, quantum networks
must contend with a more opaque form of fragility.
Photon loss, decoherence, and channel noise can silently
degrade quantum states without immediate visible
signs.

To address this, cross-layer diagnostics deploy a combination of classical and quantum measurements to monitor channel health continuously. Tools such as quantum bit error rate (QBER) estimation and photon counting statistics paint a detailed picture of the network's fidelity.

Sophisticated algorithms correlate these metrics with
classical network logs, identifying faults ranging from
fiber bends to hardware malfunctions. This cross-
domain awareness enables prompt remediation and
adaptive routing decisions that preserve quantum
integrity while maintaining classical throughput.

Early Testbeds

Insights gleaned from pioneering deployments
illuminate the path forward. Campus and metropolitan-
scale testbeds have demonstrated various hybrid
architectures in real-world conditions, revealing both
promise and pitfalls.

For example, university networks have established

quantum key distribution links intertwined with existing Ethernet and optical infrastructures, validating overlay and tandem approaches. These setups highlight practical challenges such as environmental fluctuations affecting quantum channels and synchronization issues in sprawling topologies.

Moreover, these testbeds foster collaboration among academic institutions, industry players, and standards bodies, accelerating innovation and providing invaluable feedback loops that refine both technology and practice.

Standards Initiatives

Standardization efforts are vital for interoperability and wider adoption. Consortia and working groups— such as the Internet Engineering Task Force's (IETF) Quantum Internet Research Group, and the International Telecommunication Union's (ITU) focus on quantum networks—drive the formulation of common protocols, interfaces, and performance metrics.

By establishing clear definitions for quantum-safe encryption, entanglement management, and error handling, these initiatives reduce fragmentation and encourage vendor-neutral integration. Standards also provide authoritative guidelines for security certification, compliance, and future-proofing.

As quantum networking progresses from experimental to commercial phases, these collaborative endeavors ensure that complicated architectures dissolve into accessible, scalable solutions benefiting the broader ecosystem.

Integration Best Practices

Realizing hybrid networks at scale involves careful planning to migrate legacy infrastructure. Best practices recommend a staged approach: starting with overlay models to isolate quantum links for early learning, progressively introducing tandem connections to leverage existing routing and management systems, and finally evolving toward integrated networks as technology matures.

Fiber characterization is paramount to identify channels suitable for quantum signals, accompanied by upgrading classical amplifiers and switches to quantum-compatible variants as needed. Training operational personnel in the nuances of quantum protocols and hardware is equally critical, fostering a culture of vigilance and adaptability.

Furthermore, security audits must extend beyond classical safeguards to encompass quantum-specific vulnerabilities, ensuring that the theoretical gains in quantum communication translate to robust real-world protections.

Unifying Reliability and Security

Uniting classical and quantum networks is a symphony of technological finesse and conceptual innovation. By weaving together proven reliability and scalability of classical systems with the unparalleled security and functionality promised by quantum communication, hybrid networks offer a compelling vision for the future.

This fusion demands that engineers and scientists think beyond traditional boundaries, embracing new materials, protocols, and operational paradigms. Every photon multiplexed alongside terabits of classical data, every timing pulse calibrated to attoseconds, every software stack coordinating these elements brings us closer to a global communication fabric that is not only faster and more efficient but fundamentally more secure.

In blending classical resilience with quantum subtlety, the foundation is laid for a new era where information flows freely, confidently, and with unprecedented trust-worthiness.

2.6 Quantum Internet Versus Classical Internet

The classical Internet, a marvel of modern engineering and human ingenuity, has shaped how we communicate, work, and entertain ourselves. Meanwhile, the quantum Internet, still in its infancy, proposes a fundamentally different approach to networking—one rooted not in routing packets of bits but in distributing the delicate and enigmatic resource of quantum entanglement. To appreciate the transformative potential—and the challenges—of quantum networks, it is essential to compare these two architectures on multiple fronts: their design paradigms, security frameworks, performance characteristics, scalability, interoperability, and envisioned applications.

Architectural Paradigms

At the heart of the classical Internet lies an architecture built around end-to-end packet switching. Data is chopped into manageable packets, each independently routed through an intricate labyrinth of routers and switches, converging at their destination to reassemble the original message. This layer-cake of protocols—TCP/IP, HTTP, DNS—provides robustness and flexibility, enabling everything from email to video streaming.

In stark contrast, the quantum Internet hinges on entanglement-based state distribution. Rather than sending quantum information as packets, the network establishes entangled pairs of quantum bits (qubits) between nodes. These entangled states serve as

53

the ephemeral threads linking remote quantum systems, allowing phenomena such as quantum teleportation and distributed quantum computing. Crucially, direct transmission of qubits over large distances is severely limited by noise and loss in optical fibers, so entanglement swapping via intermediate nodes becomes essential. Thus, quantum repeaters replace classical routers, creating a dynamic web of entanglement rather than fixed data paths.

This fundamental difference in data handling reshapes network design: classical networks prioritize packet forwarding and error correction, while quantum networks must create, preserve, and manage fragile quantum correlations across vast distances.

Security Models

Security in classical networks typically rests on computational hardness assumptions. Cryptographic protocols like RSA and elliptic-curve cryptography rely on problems such as factoring large numbers or discrete logarithms being infeasible to solve in reasonable time by current computers. This paradigm, while effective thus far, is threatened by the advent of sufficiently powerful quantum computers, which can break these assumptions efficiently.

Quantum networks, however, offer the tantalizing promise of information-theoretic security—guarantees that hold regardless of an adversary's computational power. Quantum key distribution (QKD), for instance, leverages the laws of quantum mechanics to detect eavesdropping directly, because measurement disturbs quantum states in a detectable way. This means keys exchanged over quantum links are provably secure against any interception or manipulation.

Yet, this elevated security model requires sophisticated

hardware and infrastructure, placing it currently beyond ubiquitous deployment. Still, as quantum computing edges closer to practical reality, the quantum Internet's ability to underpin unbreakable encryption is a compelling driver for its development.

Performance Considerations

In classical networks, throughput and latency are the key performance metrics. Decades of engineering optimized bandwidth availability and minimized delays. While errors occur in transmission, robust protocols and error correction efficiently keep data integrity high. Today's Internet supports trillions of packets daily across global fiber-optic backbones with millisecond latencies that enable streaming, gaming, and real-time collaboration.

Quantum networks face different performance challenges. Establishing high-fidelity entanglement is a slow and fragile process. Quantum states are vulnerable to decoherence and losses, translating into notably higher error rates and lower effective throughput compared to classical data channels. Repetitive entanglement attempts and purification protocols introduce latency, and error correction in the quantum domain remains experimentally challenging.

However, the measure of success here is not raw data speed but the ability to distribute entanglement reliably and securely, which will enable applications classical networks cannot match. The quest to optimize these trade-offs drives active research into materials, devices, and protocols to coax quantum networks towards practical viability.

Scalability Trade-Offs

Scaling the classical Internet has been a monumental task, involving ever-increasing routing table sizes,

hierarchical addressing schemes, and distributed
control to manage the exponentially growing number
of devices. The flexibility of packet switching allows
dynamic adaptation to network conditions and varying
traffic patterns.

Quantum networks, constrained by the fragility of
qubits and entanglement, face different scalability
hurdles. Entanglement distribution across many nodes
requires careful orchestration and synchronization
of quantum repeaters, which still must be reliably
engineered. Unlike classical routers, quantum repeaters
must maintain coherence and perform quantum error
correction, both of which become more demanding as
the network grows.

Moreover, the no-cloning theorem forbids simple signal
amplification, a mainstay of classical network scalability.
These features force quantum networks to explore novel
architectures, often hybridizing quantum and classical
channels, to scale beyond localized laboratory setups to
metropolitan and ultimately global spans.

Interoperability Requirements

A fully functional Internet thrives on standardized protocols and seamless interoperability. For classical networks, decades of international collaboration have produced universally adopted standards governing everything from physical layer signaling to high-level application protocols.

The quantum Internet, currently a patchwork of
competing approaches and prototypes, must likewise
coalesce around shared standards to enable mixed-
domain networking. This includes protocols for
entanglement generation, swapping, routing, error
correction, and integration with classical control signals.
Interoperability challenges also encompass hardware

heterogeneity—from trapped ions to nitrogen-vacancy centers and photonic systems—and managing the interface between quantum and classical layers.

Emerging standards efforts seek to facilitate this integration, aiming for hybrid networks where quantum devices coexist and interoperate with classical infrastructure, ensuring gradual evolution rather than disruptive replacement.

Use-Case Scenarios

The classical Internet serves a vast spectrum of purposes, from mundane email and social media to critical infrastructure control and cloud computing. The quantum Internet, by contrast, promises transformative applications where classical networks fall short.

Secure finance is an early and compelling use case: banks and governmental agencies implementing QKD can guarantee confidential communications immune to future quantum computing attacks. Distributed quantum sensing offers unprecedented measurement precision by harnessing entanglement-enhanced correlations across sensor networks, with potential in navigation and environmental monitoring. Quantum cloud computing envisions remote users accessing quantum processors through entangled links, exploiting quantum algorithms without the need to own a quantum computer.

These specialized applications foreshadow a complementary coexistence: classical networks will continue handling high-volume, general-purpose data traffic, while quantum networks provide enhanced security and novel computational paradigms.

Transition Roadmap

The path from today's isolated quantum links to a

pervasive quantum Internet is a multi-stage journey. Initial deployments focus on point-to-point QKD over short distances, often within metropolitan areas or between trusted nodes. Parallel efforts develop quantum repeaters and error-correcting modules to extend range and reliability.

Subsequently, regional quantum backbones will emerge, connecting multiple nodes via entanglement swapping chains and integrating classical network support. The final stage envisions a global quantum Internet, where quantum routers dynamically manage entanglement resources across continents, enabling worldwide secure communication and distributed quantum computing.

Each progression depends on advances in materials, device engineering, network protocols, and user applications, demanding coordinated efforts across research, industry, and regulatory bodies.

Standardization Efforts

Recognizing that no communication technology succeeds without standards, leading organizations have begun shaping the quantum Internet's foundation. The Internet Engineering Task Force (IETF) and the Institute of Electrical and Electronics Engineers (IEEE) host working groups exploring quantum network protocols and interface standards. Likewise, international bodies such as the International Telecommunication Union (ITU) collaborate on spectrum allocation and optical fiber standards suitable for quantum signals.

These efforts address topics such as quantum link layer definitions, entanglement distribution control, synchronization mechanisms, and data format specifications. By defining open, interoperable frameworks early, these bodies aim to accelerate innovation, investment, and eventual deployment of quantum networking technologies worldwide.

Future Outlook

While many quantum Internet components remain experimental, rapid progress signals that functional quantum networks may emerge within the coming decade. Achieving robust quantum repeaters and scalable multi-node entanglement will mark pivotal milestones. Ongoing improvements in integrated photonics, quantum memory, and error correction fuel optimism for overcoming current limitations.

Beyond technical breakthroughs, economic and societal drivers—ranging from cybersecurity imperatives to burgeoning quantum-enabled services—will shape deployment timelines. The interplay with classical networks will likely persist for decades, blending mature infrastructure with quantum enhancements.

As with the classical Internet decades ago, broad adoption may unfold in waves, seeding a transformative digital fabric redefining secure communication, computation, and sensing in the 21st century.

Comparing classical and quantum Internet architectures reveals a profound shift in how networks function and what they enable. The classical Internet's packet-switched, computationally secured, high-throughput design contrasts sharply with the quantum Internet's entanglement-based, information-theoretic secured, latency-constrained architecture. Each paradigm faces its own scalability and interoperability challenges, but together they promise a future where quantum and classical networks coexist, complementing each other's strengths. While widespread quantum networking is still emerging, its specialized applications herald a new era of ultra-secure communication and distributed quantum services that enrich and transcend the foundations laid by the classical Internet.

Chapter 3

The Building Blocks of Quantum Networks

This chapter examines the essential physical and architectural components required to build scalable quantum communication systems. We start with the properties and limits of quantum channels over fiber and free space, then explore the design of nodes and repeaters that extend links across long distances. Next, we detail photon-based encoding, generation, and detection methods, followed by the critical interfaces that tie quantum hardware to classical control and routing. We then survey existing prototype networks and testbeds, and conclude with an overview of quantum memory technologies for buffering and retrieving quantum information.

3.1   Quantum Channels

Quantum networks rely fundamentally on channels that can ferry qubits—quantum bits of information— between distant nodes without erasing the delicate quantum properties they embody. These *quantum channels* act as invisible highways for superposition and entanglement to traverse space. Unlike classical communication lines, they must maintain coherence, the fragile quantum correlation that gives qubits their power, throughout the journey. This sets stringent demands on their design and operation: minimal loss,

low noise, and preservation of quantum states amid
environmental perturbations.

A principal medium for quantum channels is optical
fiber, long familiar for classical telecommunications
but with features particularly suited to the quantum
realm. Most quantum networks employ *single-mode
fibers*, whose slender core confines light tightly, ensuring
photons travel with minimal modal distortion. These
fibers boast *low-loss windows*—specific wavelength
bands where absorption and scattering are naturally
minimal—most notably near 1.55 micrometers, tailored
by the silica glass composition. Yet propagation through
fiber is not without challenge; *chromatic dispersion* arises
because photons of slightly differing wavelengths travel
at varying speeds, potentially spreading out quantum
pulses and undermining timing precision crucial to
quantum information protocols.

Loss in optical fibers primarily stems from three
mechanisms. *Absorption* occurs when photons transfer
energy to impurities or the glass itself, effectively
vanishing from the quantum channel. *Scattering*,
especially Rayleigh scattering, redirects photons
randomly out of the guided mode, further depleting the
signal. Lastly, physical handling introduces losses by
bending the fiber, where tight curves allow light to leak
out. Notably, these losses accumulate exponentially
with distance, severely limiting how far qubits can
travel without amplification—a vexing problem since
amplification itself tends to destroy quantum coherence.

The signal decay as photons traverse a fiber of length
d is elegantly captured by the exponential attenuation
formula,

$$I(d) = I_0 e^{-\alpha d},$$

where I_0 is the initial photon intensity and α is the attenuation coefficient, typically measured in inverse kilometers. This formula reveals how even small losses per kilometer swiftly reduce the surviving photon count, forcing the use of quantum repeaters or alternate channels for long distances.

Complementing fiber, *free-space quantum links* leverage line-of-sight optical channels, beaming photons through the atmosphere or even to satellites. These links hold promise for global quantum communication, circumventing fiber's physical constraints. However, free-space propagation entails its own set of challenges. Photons spread due to *beam divergence*, requiring careful control of beam shape and size so the receiver collects sufficient light. Achieving precise *pointing accuracy* is no trivial task, especially over hundreds of kilometers or in moving platforms like satellites, where vibration and atmospheric refraction can cause jitter.

The atmosphere itself acts as a dynamic adversary. *Turbulence* induced by temperature and pressure fluctuations randomly distorts the beam wavefront, leading to scintillation—flickering and intensity variations that degrade signal quality. Atmospheric *absorption* by water vapor, ozone, and other gases reduces transmission further, while weather conditions such as fog, rain, or clouds impose unpredictable interruptions. Yet, well-chosen wavelengths and adaptive optics can mitigate many of these effects, ensuring a robust quantum connection under favorable conditions.

All these environmental interactions inevitably couple the flying qubits to extraneous degrees of freedom, introducing *channel noise* and *decoherence*—the enemies of quantum fidelity. Noise manifests as random perturbations affecting the qubit's state, causing errors in transmitted information. Decoherence progressively dimin-

ishes quantum correlations, making entanglement fragile over distance. Balancing the conflicting demands of
long-range reach and coherent preservation shapes the
engineering of quantum channel systems.

The ultimate capacity of a quantum channel—the rate at
which it can reliably transmit qubits—is limited by these
losses and noises. Quantum information theory establishes theoretical bounds, such as the *quantum capacity*,
marking the highest achievable rate under ideal error
correction. In practice, trade-offs arise between distance,
rate, and error tolerance, guiding protocols for encoding,
error detection, and entanglement purification.

To quantify a quantum channel's error performance, the
Quantum Bit Error Rate (QBER) serves as a key metric:

$$\text{QBER} = \frac{N_{\text{error}}}{N_{\text{total}}},$$

where N_{error} is the count of erroneous bits detected, and
N_{total} the total transmitted. Low QBER values are imperative for secure quantum key distribution and depend-
able quantum computing, as high error rates erode trust
in the transmitted quantum information.

The choice between optical fiber and free-space channels
depends heavily on deployment scenarios and technical
constraints. The table below summarizes their principal characteristics, highlighting the trade-offs in loss profiles, typical operational range, and practical considerations.

Property	Optical Fiber	Free-Space Link
Loss Mechanisms	Absorption, Rayleigh scattering, bending loss	Atmospheric absorption, turbulence, beam divergence
Low-Loss Windows	Near 1.55 μm wavelength	Atmospheric transmission windows near 800–1550 nm
Typical Range	Up to $\sim$100 km without repeaters	Tens to hundreds of km; satellite links enable global range
Environmental Sensitivity	Protected inside cables; stable	Highly variable; subject to weather and atmospheric conditions
Deployment Complexity	Requires physical infrastructure	Requires line-of-sight and active pointing systems
Coherence Preservation	High if losses controlled	Challenging due to turbulence and pointing errors

Table 3.1: Comparison of optical fiber and free-space quantum channels

Together, optical fiber and free-space quantum channels form the backbone of emerging quantum networks— each bringing unique strengths and obstacles. Fibers offer a mature, robust medium ideal for urban and suburban networks, whereas free-space links hold the key to scaling quantum connectivity beyond terrestrial limits. Progress in materials, photonics, and adaptive technologies continues to push these channels closer to the ideal of seamless, high-fidelity quantum communication over vast distances.

3.2 Quantum Nodes and Repeaters

Quantum networks promise the ability to share information with unprecedented security and computational power by leveraging the mysterious phenomenon of *entanglement*. However, entanglement is a delicate thread, fragile over distance and susceptible to the losses and noise of the physical world. Unlike classical signals, which can be simply amplified to travel farther, quantum information cannot be cloned or boosted without destroying its essential properties. This is where quantum nodes and repeaters come into play: they form the backbone of a network designed to generate, extend, and maintain entanglement across vast distances.

At the heart of this architecture lie *quantum nodes*, specialized units responsible for orchestrating the flow of quantum information. Their primary roles are threefold: generating entangled pairs of quantum bits (qubits), storing quantum states temporarily, and performing measurements that enable entanglement to be swapped or purified. Consider quantum nodes as diligent conductors in a vast orchestra, each ensuring their section is perfectly tuned and their cues precisely timed.

To accomplish these functions, nodes incorporate several critical hardware modules.

- *Photon interfaces* act as translators between matter-based qubits (often represented by atoms, ions, or defects in solids) and photons, the carriers of quantum information over optical fibers. These interfaces must efficiently create and detect single photons while preserving their quantum states.

- *Quantum memories* within the node provide short-term storage for qubits, allowing synchronization of operations and flexible timing in establishing links. Unlike classical memory, quantum memories require isolation from environmental disturbances and precise control to maintain coherence.

- *Classical controllers* coordinate the protocols

running across the network, sending and receiving classical signals that herald successful entanglement attempts or trigger further operations. This marriage of quantum and classical hardware underpins the complex dance of entanglement distribution.

The first step in extending quantum links involves establishing an *elementary link*—a direct entanglement between adjacent nodes. Various protocols achieve this by generating entangled photon pairs at a central source or at one node, then distributing one photon to each node across the link. Upon successful detection events, signaled by classical communication, nodes confirm the creation of an entangled pair. Because photon transmission is lossy and probabilistic, multiple attempts may be necessary before an elementary entangled pair is ready and stored in quantum memories at both ends.

The magic of quantum repeaters unfolds when these elementary links are stitched together using the *entanglement swapping* protocol. Imagine two adjacent links, each sharing an entangled pair between their endpoints. If the intermediate node performs a joint measurement on its two qubits—one from each link— it effectively projects the distant end nodes into an entangled state without any direct interaction. This nonlocal operation forms a longer entangled connection, extending the reach of quantum communication beyond individual links. Iterating this process over multiple nodes can create entanglement spanning hundreds or thousands of kilometers.

Not all quantum repeaters are created equal. Their classification into *generations* and types reflects differences in hardware complexity, security assumptions, and performance. The simplest *trusted repeaters* function almost like classical relays: they measure, store, and retransmit quantum information, but require trustworthiness because they access the underlying quantum data. On the other hand, *untrusted repeaters* rely solely on entanglement swapping and purification, never accessing the quantum information directly, thus preserving end-to-end security.

Between these extremes, three generations of quantum repeaters have emerged conceptually. First-generation repeaters use heralded entanglement generation and swapping with additional *purification* steps to boost the quality, or fidelity, of entanglement amid noise and losses. Second-generation architectures introduce quantum error correction codes, reducing reliance on purification but demanding more sophisticated hardware. The third generation envisions fully fault-tolerant, error-corrected quantum communication, enabling rapid and robust long-distance transmission, though this remains a formidable experimental challenge.

Purification and distillation are vital processes in this landscape. As signals travel through imperfect fibers and components, the entangled states degrade, reducing their usefulness for quantum protocols. By combining multiple low-fidelity entangled pairs through clever measurement and classical communication, purification extracts fewer but higher-quality entangled pairs. This tradeoff is essential to maintaining the integrity of entanglement over extended repeater chains, allowing quantum networks to surpass classical limits.

Crucially, coordination among nodes demands exquisite *synchronization*. Because entanglement generation and swapping rely on detecting photons and performing joint measurements, timing jitter or delays can corrupt the delicate quantum states.

Techniques to synchronize clocks and signals to sub-nanosecond precision underpin the successful operation of repeaters, ensuring that photons from different sources arrive simultaneously and classical messages confirm outcomes without harmful latency.

Assessing the performance of quantum nodes and repeaters involves balancing several metrics. *Throughput* measures the rate at which high-fidelity entangled pairs emerge from the network, reflecting how quickly users can exchange quantum information. *Latency* captures the delay between initiating a communication request and receiving entanglement, shaped by the probabilistic nature of generation and classical signaling. Perhaps most pivotal is *fidelity*—the overlap between the real entangled state and an ideal one—which determines the reliability of quantum protocols running on top of the network.

Despite their promise, physical implementation of quantum nodes and repeaters faces considerable challenges. Achieving *thermal stability* is vital, as even tiny temperature fluctuations can cause shifts in frequencies and coupling efficiencies, undermining coherent operations. Integrating diverse components—photon sources, memories, detectors, and electronics—into compact, scalable packages remains an ongoing engineering feat. Moreover, quantum memories must balance long coherence times with the ability to write and retrieve qubits quickly, demanding advances in materials and control techniques. Resource demands, including the need for cryogenic cooling or vacuum environments, add further complexity to real-world deployment.

Yet, as experimentalists and theorists collaborate, breakthroughs continue to push the boundaries. Quantum nodes and repeaters are moving from

laboratory curiosities toward functional elements of
future quantum networks, enabling secure communication, distributed quantum computing, and sensing
applications once thought impossible. Through
a sophisticated interplay of hardware modules,
communication protocols, and error management,
these components weave together the fragile threads
of entanglement into robust fabrics connecting distant
points.

Ultimately, quantum nodes and repeaters transform the
ephemeral properties of quantum states into practical infrastructure, extending the remarkable phenomenon of
entanglement across physical space. Their development
not only challenges our engineering ingenuity but also
reshapes our notions of connectivity, privacy, and information itself in an increasingly quantum world.

3.3 Photons as Information Carriers

Photons—quanta of light—have long been regarded
as the quintessential messengers in both classical
and quantum realms. Their unique physical properties
make them extraordinarily well-suited to carry quantum
information, or *qubits*, between distant points. Unlike
electrons or atoms, photons do not easily interact with
their environment, allowing information to remain
uncorrupted over long distances. This section explores
why photons stand out as ideal qubit carriers, the
elegant ways quantum information is encoded onto
them, the technologies powering their generation and
detection, and the practical challenges inherent in their
use.

Advantages of Photons

The prowess of photons as qubit carriers begins with

their remarkable resilience to decoherence—the loss or corruption of quantum information. Photons interact so minimally with their surroundings that quantum states encoded upon them can traverse kilometers of optical fiber or through free space without substantial degradation. This minimal interaction contrasts sharply with matter-based qubits, whose susceptibility to environmental disturbances demands extreme cooling or isolation.

Another pragmatic advantage is their compatibility with room-temperature operation. Unlike many quantum systems requiring cryogenic apparatus, photons can be manipulated, routed, and detected reliably in everyday laboratory and industrial settings. Moreover, the existing global telecommunications infrastructure—built around fiber-optic cables—naturally accommodates photons as information carriers, facilitating seamless integration of quantum communication protocols into current networks.

These combined attributes—robustness against noise, ambient operation, and fiber compatibility—position photons as unrivaled conduits for transmitting quantum information across scalable distances.

Encoding Quantum Information onto Photons

Conveying a quantum bit using a photon involves cleverly assigning its quantum states to represent logical $|0\rangle$ and $|1\rangle$. Several encoding schemes are popular, differing in technical feasibility and resilience to transmission impairments.

Polarization Encoding

Arguably the most intuitive way to encode a qubit onto a photon is via its polarization—the orientation of its electric field oscillations. Horizontal polarization

$(|H\rangle)$ and vertical polarization $(|V\rangle)$ naturally
correspond to the computational basis states $|0\rangle$
and $|1\rangle$. Superpositions of these states can represent
any general qubit, embodying the hallmark quantum
property of being in multiple states simultaneously.

Polarization encoding benefits from easy manipulation
using wave plates and polarizing beam splitters, as
well as efficient detection methods. It is a preferred
method in free-space quantum communication and
short-distance laboratory setups. However, when
photons travel through optical fibers, birefringence and
environmental fluctuations can rotate the polarization
state unpredictably, thereby introducing errors.

Time-Bin Encoding

To overcome polarization's susceptibility in fibers, time-
bin encoding offers an elegant alternative. Instead of
orientation, quantum information is encoded in the photon's time of arrival. A qubit might be defined by an
"early" pulse representing $|0\rangle$ and a "late" pulse repre-
senting $|1\rangle$. Superpositions correspond to coherent com-
binations of these pulses.

Time-bin qubits are remarkably robust against
disturbances in optical fiber channels because timing
remains more stable than polarization over long
distances and varying environmental conditions. This
method requires interferometric setups to prepare
and measure the quantum states, but its resistance
to channel noise has made it a workhorse in practical
quantum networks.

Frequency Encoding

Another sophisticated technique encodes qubits in
the spectral composition of photons. Here, different
frequency modes or wavelengths are assigned logical

states. For example, a photon occupying a particular narrow frequency band corresponds to $|0\rangle$, while a photon at a distinct band maps to $|1\rangle$.

Superpositions occur through coherent spectral shaping—where the photon resides simultaneously in multiple frequency components. Frequency encoding facilitates wavelength division multiplexing, allowing many qubits to be transmitted simultaneously along a single fiber by using different channels. This multiplexing capability can dramatically enhance the communication capacity of quantum networks.

Each encoding strategy involves trade-offs related to ease of generation, stability in transmission, and complexity of detection, which we will explore in greater detail shortly.

Generating Single Photons and Qubits

Producing true single photons on demand is a non-trivial technical challenge central to photonic quantum information. Several technologies have emerged to address this, each with distinct advantages.

One widely used method relies on spontaneous parametric down-conversion (SPDC) in nonlinear crystals. In this process, a high-energy "pump" photon spontaneously splits into two lower-energy photons, known as signal and idler. Detecting one photon heralds the presence of its twin, allowing for probabilistic but highly reliable single-photon generation. Although conceptually straightforward, SPDC sources emit photons randomly in time, necessitating additional multiplexing strategies to approximate on-demand emission.

Quantum dots—nanoscale semiconductor structures—offer an alternative capable of true on-demand photon emission. When excited by a laser pulse, a quantum dot can emit a single photon with well-defined properties. These engineered sources promise scalability and integration with photonic circuits, although maintaining uniformity and controlling decoherence phenomena remain active areas of research.

Other heralded single-photon sources include atom-cavity systems and color centers in diamond, but SPDC crystals and quantum dots currently dominate practical implementations.

Detecting Single Photons

Equally important to encoding and generation is the reliable detection of single photons. Two detector types stand out: avalanche photodiodes (APDs) and superconducting nanowire single-photon detectors (SNSPDs).

APDs operate at near-room temperature and exploit an avalanche multiplication process, generating an easily measurable electrical signal upon photon absorption. They are widely available, cost-effective, and well suited for many quantum optics experiments. However, APDs suffer from limited detection efficiencies and higher dark counts (false positives).

SNSPDs, in contrast, are cryogenically cooled devices constructed from ultrathin superconducting wires. Upon photon absorption, a tiny region temporarily loses superconductivity, causing a measurable voltage pulse. SNSPDs provide exceptional efficiency, low timing jitter, and extremely low dark count rates, making them ideal for demanding quantum communication tasks. Their main drawback is the complexity and cost of cryogenic operation.

Challenges: Loss and Indistinguishability

No exploration of photonic qubits would be complete without mentioning two fundamental challenges: photon loss and indistinguishability.

Loss arises as photons are absorbed or scattered during transmission through fibers or free space. These losses reduce signal strength and probability of successful qubit detection. While classical amplifiers solve this issue for ordinary signals, quantum information cannot be cloned or amplified directly without destroying coherence—a constraint known as the *no-cloning theorem*. Thus, managing loss demands careful engineering of sources, transmission media, and detectors, as well as techniques like quantum repeaters.

Indistinguishability refers to the degree to which photons produced from different sources are identical in all quantum properties (frequency, timing, polarization, etc.). High indistinguishability is crucial for two-photon interference effects, which underpin many quantum communication protocols and entanglement distribution schemes. Timing jitter, spectral variations, and mode mismatch degrade this property, reducing the success rates of quantum gates and teleportation.

Boosting Communication Rates: Multiplexing

To overcome probabilistic photon generation and loss, multiplexing techniques have become vital. Multiplexing involves sending multiple qubits simultaneously across distinct degrees of freedom, effectively increasing the quantum key rate and bandwidth.

Spatial multiplexing uses parallel optical paths or fiber cores, each carrying independent qubits. Temporal multiplexing sends a rapid sequence of photons separated by well-defined time intervals. Wavelength multiplexing exploits different frequency channels within the fiber's spectral window, often combined with frequency encoding.

These approaches, especially when complemented by multiplexed single-photon sources and detectors, can significantly enhance the throughput and reliability of quantum communication networks, edging quantum technologies closer to practical deployment.

Encoding Method	Strengths	Challenges
Polarization	Intuitive, easy manipulation	Sensitive to fiber birefringence
Time-Bin	Robust in fibers, stable transmission	Requires interferometers for encoding/decoding
Frequency	Enables wavelength multiplexing	Demands precise spectral control and filtering

Table 3.2: Comparative overview of photon encoding methods

Each encoding scheme carves a distinctive niche within the broader landscape of quantum photonics, and practical implementations often combine multiple methods to optimize performance.

By harnessing the unique advantages of photons—their minimal interactions, room-temperature operability, and compatibility with existing fiber infrastructure—quantum information science continues to build toward scalable, reliable, and high-speed quantum communication. The interplay between encoding methods, source and detector technologies, and innovative multiplexing strategies ensure that photons remain at the heart of quantum networks for years to come.

3.4 Interfaces Between Quantum and Classical Worlds

The promise of quantum technologies hinges not only on the mysterious behavior of qubits but crucially on how these quantum systems connect, interact, and co-exist with the classical devices that surround us. This quantum-classical interface forms the backbone of practical quantum hardware, routing, control, and network management. Understanding how these layers communicate reveals the delicate dance between two fundamentally different realms: the fragile superpositions of quantum states and the robust, deterministic classical signals that command them.

At the heart of this interface lie *classical control channels*, which serve as the vital information highways coordinating quantum operations. Although quantum states encode information in ways inaccessible to classical intuition, managing these states demands classical signals to initiate, modulate, and interpret quantum processes. For example, classical channels deliver microwave pulses to superconducting qubits, time laser shots for trapped-ion systems, or set voltage biases for quantum dots. These channels ensure that quantum gates activate with precise timing, and measurement results are promptly relayed back, acting as the nervous system of the quantum hardware.

Bridging the electromagnetic divide between quantum devices—often operating at microwave or radio frequencies—and optical fiber networks requires *electro-optic transducers*. These remarkable components convert electrical or microwave signals into optical quantum states that photons can carry over long distances with minimal loss. The challenge here is preserving fragile quantum coherence during conversion, akin to translating poetry without losing its meaning. Various approaches—mechanical, electro-optic, or magneto-optic—are under active research, striving to efficiently transform quantum information between microwave resonators and telecommunication wavelengths. Such hybrid systems pave the way for quantum data to traverse existing fiber-optic infrastructure, linking distant quantum nodes.

Once quantum and classical signals coexist, they demand sophisticated *signal routing and switching* systems designed to handle both types of traffic gracefully. Hybrid switches direct quantum photons and classical control pulses alike, often using time-multiplexed or wavelength-selective schemes. Unlike classical networks, quantum switches must preserve coherence and avoid measurement-induced collapse. This subtle requirement inspires designs that minimize loss, decoherence, and crosstalk while still offering flexibility and scalability. For instance, integrated photonic circuits can route single photons using microelectromechanical elements or nonlinear optical effects, enabling dynamic and programmable quantum networks.

Synchronization and timing form the rhythmic heartbeat of these hybrid networks, especially when operations depend on delicate quantum interferences or sequential measurement-driven protocols. *Clock distribution systems* ensure sub-nanosecond alignment of events across disparate nodes, a necessity since even slight delays can scramble quantum coherence or cause feed-forward operations to falter. Achieving such precision often involves stabilized optical frequency combs or ultra-low jitter electronic timing units delivering synchronized triggers. This ultra-precise coordination is critical when quantum operations on separate nodes

combine to enact distributed algorithms or error
correction cycles.

Measurement in quantum networks is more than
just reading out a qubit's state; it frequently triggers
immediate reconfiguration of subsequent quantum
gates or transmission routes. Known as *measurement
and feed-forward,* this process uses classical detector
outcomes to dynamically control quantum operations
in real-time. For example, a photon detection event on
one node may herald the successful entanglement of
distant qubits, prompting another device to perform a
conditional gate. This delicate feedback loop demands
classical communication channels with minimal
latency and protocols that reconcile probabilistic
quantum events with deterministic classical commands,
thereby enabling adaptive and fault-tolerant quantum
computation.

Managing this interplay of quantum and classical
resources requires a sophisticated *network management
plane,* a software layer that allocates and schedules
both quantum and classical elements. Unlike classical
networks where data flow dominates, quantum
networks must juggle scarce entanglement resources,
qubit decoherence windows, and classical control
bandwidth simultaneously. This management software
coordinates routing, error mitigation, and resource
sharing, often aiming to abstract quantum hardware
complexities from higher-level applications. The goal
is a seamless orchestration where quantum operations
proceed transparently, guided by intelligent classical
oversight.

Security concerns, naturally paramount in quantum networks, extend to their classical interfaces. *Interface security* must guard classical control channels against side-
channel exploits and malicious interference that could

indirectly compromise quantum operations. Since quantum devices rely on classical signals for timing and control, an adversary manipulating these signals may disrupt quantum protocols without directly attacking the qubits. This reality demands encryption, authentication, and intrusion detection tailored to classical links, preserving the integrity of the entire hybrid system.

As networks scale from a handful of quantum devices to potentially thousands, *scalability considerations* become paramount. Interface modules must be designed for modular replication, allowing addition of nodes without exponential complexity growth. Architectures often favor distributed control with standardized interface units, minimizing wiring complexity and thermal loads. Innovations such as multiplexed control pulses, integrated photonics, and cryogenic classical controllers help manage scaling challenges, ensuring that increased node counts do not overwhelm interface capabilities.

Driving this technological evolution is an emerging framework of *standards and protocols* dedicated to quantum-classical interoperability. Unlike the well-established classical internet protocols, quantum networks require fresh specifications spanning timing synchronization, resource reservation, error reporting, and security policies that respect quantum constraints. International consortia and research alliances are actively defining these guidelines to foster compatibility across diverse hardware platforms and vendors, ultimately enabling a coherent global quantum infrastructure.

Across this complex landscape, best practices have begun to crystallize for seamless integration. Prioritizing low-latency and low-loss interfaces, combining robust classical error control with quantum error mitigation, and employing modular architectures that separate quantum cores from classical control electronics all prove crucial. Interoperability efforts emphasize open interfaces and well-defined abstraction layers, enabling independent development of quantum and classical subsystems yet maintaining tight coordination. Together, these design principles ensure that the seemingly disparate classical and quantum worlds merge into a functional, reliable quantum ecosystem.

In essence, the interface between quantum and classical worlds is neither an afterthought nor a mere technical detail but a profound frontier where physics, engineering, and information science converge. It is here that the promise of quantum technologies becomes tangible, transforming delicate quantum phenomena into usable, controlled, and scalable systems supporting computations, communications, and sensing beyond today's capabilities. The success of quantum technology depends on mastering this interface, connecting the ethereal quantum realm with the grounded classical infrastructure that shapes our technological world.

3.5 Current Prototypes and Testbeds

Quantum communication, once a theoretical curiosity, has evolved into a flourishing field grounded in experimental reality. Today's landscape is peppered with a variety of pioneering prototypes and testbeds that showcase how quantum principles can reshape the way we transmit information. These early-stage implementations provide vital insights—both technological and conceptual—that bridge the gap between laboratory experiments and real-world quantum networks. By examining where we stand, both in terms of infrastructure and performance, we gain a clearer picture of the exciting challenges and opportunities ahead.

Metropolitan and Campus Testbeds

The first step beyond isolated experiments involved creating quantum communication channels spanning city blocks or entire campuses. These metropolitan and university networks typically rely on optical fibers, leveraging existing telecommunication infrastructure to connect multiple sites. For instance, the well-known DARPA Quantum Network, established in the early 2000s around Boston, linked Harvard, Boston University, and the Massachusetts Institute of Technology with quantum channels that demonstrated secure key exchange over tens of kilometers.

Similarly, Europe's SECOQC (Secure Communication based on Quantum Cryptography) project interconnected fiber networks in Vienna, testing quantum key distribution (QKD) protocols in practical urban settings. These networks exposed crucial engineering challenges—such as variances in fiber quality and ambient noise—while validating that metropolitan-scale quantum links could indeed operate reliably amid the chaos of real city environments. Campus networks afforded controlled environments to trial different quantum protocols and error-correction techniques, pushing the boundary of how quantum signals behave when multiplexed with classical data traffic.

Satellite Demonstrations

While fiber optic networks are invaluable, their reach is ultimately limited by loss and noise accumulating over distance. To overcome this, researchers have turned their gaze skyward, exploiting the near-vacuum of space as a transmission medium. Satellite-based quantum communication represents a paradigm shift: instead of light struggling through kilometers of glass, photons can traverse the emptiness between Earth and orbit with minimal absorption.

The launch of China's Micius satellite marked a watershed moment. Operating from space to ground stations separated by thousands of kilometers, Micius successfully demonstrated entanglement distribution, quantum teleportation, and QKD at scales never before realized. These groundbreaking experiments validated the feasibility of global quantum networks extending beyond terrestrial constraints.

However, these advances come with unique hurdles: atmospheric turbulence, precise pointing and tracking of photons over vast distances, and limited satellite operation windows. Despite these, the evident successes motivate ongoing efforts to deploy constellations of quantum satellites, potentially forming a backbone for worldwide secure communication.

National Quantum Initiatives

Many governments, recognizing the strategic and economic importance of quantum technologies, have embarked on ambitious national quantum programs. These initiatives often revolve around creating quantum communication backbones that connect major cities and research centers. For example, China's Quantum Experiments at Space Scale and Earth Scale (QUESS) initiative integrates satellite and terrestrial fiber links, spanning thousands of kilometers.

In Europe, the Quantum Internet Alliance and related projects aim to establish robust intercity quantum networks, while the U.S. Department of Energy and National Institute of Standards and Technology have supported nationwide testbeds combining metropolitan fibers with research laboratories. These national efforts serve as test grounds for interoperable technologies,

protocol standardization, and the creation of a future
quantum internet—promising a secure infrastructure
for sensitive governmental, commercial, and scientific
data.

Integrated Photonic Chips

Up to now, many quantum communication components
have been bulky, delicate, and confined to laboratory
settings. However, the field is rapidly moving toward
miniaturization through integrated photonics. By
fabricating sources of quantum light, optical circuits,
and detectors on single chips—much like microchips in
classical electronics—researchers are creating compact,
stable, and scalable quantum nodes.

These integrated quantum photonic chips not only
reduce system complexity and cost but also facilitate
mass production and deployment. Companies and
research groups have demonstrated on-chip entangled
photon sources, waveguide circuits for routing quantum
signals, and superconducting nanowire detectors—all
incorporated into portable devices suitable for field
deployment. The continued progress in this arena
underpins the eventual realization of quantum repeaters
and routers, essential building blocks for long-distance
quantum networks.

Performance Benchmarks

Evaluating early testbeds' performance requires clear
metrics, revealing their practical viability and guiding
future improvements. Key rate—the speed at which
secret keys are generated—remains a central figure of
merit, as higher rates directly translate to more practical
secure communication. Alongside this, quantum bit
error rate (QBER) measures the fraction of transmitted
bits corrupted during transmission; maintaining low
QBER is vital to guarantee security.

Uptime and channel stability have also gained attention as networks transition from experimental to operational modes. Metropolitan testbeds commonly achieve key rates ranging from a few kilobits per second up to megabits, varying with distance and protocol sophistication. Satellite links, plagued by atmospheric disturbances and limited operational windows, tend to deliver lower average rates but compensate with dramatically extended reach.

Engineering Lessons Learned

The story of quantum communication is as much about navigating engineering realities as it is about physics. Real-world deployment brings environmental noise, synchronization challenges, and signal loss from fiber imperfections or atmospheric scattering. For instance, time synchronization across spatially separated nodes—critical for matching photon arrival times—has demanded innovative clock distribution methods and feedback control systems.

Loss mitigation has spurred designs for ultra-low-loss fibers, intelligent error correction, and multiplexing techniques. Active stabilization of fiber polarization and temperature control further enhance system robustness. In satellite systems, adaptive optics and precise beam steering address the microscopic jitter and distortion caused by Earth's atmosphere. These technical innovations demonstrate quantum communication's journey from fragile proof-of-concept to reliable technology.

Timeline of Key Milestones

Tracing the evolution of quantum communication testbeds illuminates the rapid pace of progress. In the 1990s, pioneering point-to-point QKD links over kilometers of fiber set the foundations. The early 2000s

saw the birth of urban quantum networks, blending
academic and commercial interests. By 2010, space-
based demonstrations began with modest satellite
experiments, culminating in record-breaking Micius
achievements around 2016–2017.

Simultaneously, integrated photonics advanced from
simple prototypes to functional quantum circuits by
the late 2010s. National projects became prominent
post-2015, coordinating large-scale deployments with
billions in funding. Each milestone represents a synergy
of quantum theory, engineering innovation, and system
integration, progressively addressing the challenges of
scale, reliability, and practicality.

Operational Insights

Operating quantum communication networks outside
laboratories reveals insights beyond raw performance
figures. Continuous operation highlights the importance of maintenance protocols for sensitive
components—lasers, detectors, and cooling systems—
that must function with minimal downtime. Automated
error alerts and adaptive calibration are now integral to
maintaining link stability.

Reliability depends not only on hardware but also on
software layers managing protocols and key distribution.
Early testbeds often experienced interruptions from
environmental factors like temperature swings or fiber
bending, prompting the development of ruggedized
hardware and dynamic compensation algorithms.
These operational experiences emphasize that quantum
networks, like their classical counterparts, must
seamlessly integrate engineering discipline with
quantum physics.

Scalability Studies

Scalability is the holy grail: whether small, proof-of-concept quantum links can evolve into mesh networks connecting dozens or hundreds of nodes across continents. Experiments testing node addition have demonstrated that networks can be extended by carefully synchronizing quantum states across newly incorporated segments. For example, metropolitan testbeds have linked multiple trusted nodes, showcasing the possibility of decentralized key distribution.

Studies on extending link length show a steep drop in quantum signal fidelity beyond certain distances due to unavoidable loss, stimulating intense research into quantum repeaters—devices capable of restoring quantum states without measurement. While full-scale repeater implementation remains elusive, testbeds exploring multiplexing techniques and new quantum memory elements lay the groundwork for long-range scalability.

Security Assessments

Finally, testbeds have served as proving grounds not only for technological capability but also for security assurances central to quantum communication's promise. Protocol robustness has been evaluated by simulated attacks—such as photon-number splitting, detector blinding, or channel manipulation—to identify vulnerabilities and adapt countermeasures.

These experimental security assessments have spurred the refinement of device-independent protocols, which rely less on assumptions about hardware trustworthiness, further strengthening guarantees. The ongoing dialogue between attackers' tactics and protocol designers' defenses underlines that quantum communication is a dynamic battlefield, where theoretical security and practical implementation continually inform each other.

This constellation of metropolitan fibers, orbital satellites, national projects, miniaturized chips, and rigorous operational testing illustrates that quantum communication is not a distant dream but a blossoming reality. The strides made in current prototypes and testbeds define a roadmap illuminated by experimental triumphs and engineered finesse, guiding the way toward a future where quantum networks underpin a new era of secure, revolutionary communication.

3.6 Quantum Memory and Storage

Quantum communication hinges on more than just sending photons securely through optical fibers or free space; it depends critically on the ability to temporarily hold and manage quantum information. This function is the raison d'être of quantum memory—a sophisticated technology designed to buffer fragile quantum states without destroying their inherent coherence. In the architecture of quantum repeaters, which extend communication distances by segmenting the channel and correcting errors at intervals, quantum memories serve as indispensable temporal anchors. They synchronize the staggered delivery of entangled photons, waiting patiently until all parts of the network are prepared to advance. Without these storages, the entire chain risks collapse from the asynchronous arrival or loss of quantum bits (qubits).

One of the more intuitive natural platforms for quantum memory derives from atomic ensembles— collections of atoms, often cooled near absolute zero or contained within warm vapor cells, that act collectively to store quantum states. When a photon enters such a medium, its quantum information is mapped not onto an individual atom but onto a collective excitation called a spin wave. This subtle distribution means the quantum state is shared among many atoms, enhancing robustness against certain types of noise. Techniques like Electromagnetically Induced Transparency (EIT) help render the medium temporarily transparent, allowing an incoming photon to be absorbed coherently while preserving its quantum features. These ensembles have demonstrated storage times ranging from microseconds to milliseconds, with room-temperature vapor cells offering practicality at the expense of shorter coherence periods compared to their ultracold counterparts.

In parallel, solid-state memories advance a markedly different approach, embedding quantum states within crystalline lattices doped with impurities such as rare-earth ions or nitrogen-vacancy (NV) centers in diamond. Rare-earth-doped crystals have a remarkable ability to trap photons as optical excitations within narrow energy levels, harnessing long-lived spin states for storage. NV centers, meanwhile, stand out for their spin properties and optical accessibility at room temperature, enabling promising quantum memories that can be integrated with photonic circuits. Their solid-state nature facilitates miniaturization and potential scalability, though challenges remain in matching optical and spectral properties with transmission channels to maximize efficiency.

At the heart of all these memory systems lie the write and read processes—protocols that translate flying qubits into stationary ones and back again without degrading their quantum essence. Writing involves coherently absorbing a photon's state into the memory, effectively imprinting its quantum information onto

the internal degrees of freedom of the medium. This
demands carefully tuned interactions to prevent loss
or decoherence. Retrieval is equally delicate: the
stored excitation must be converted back into a photon
on demand, with precise control over timing and
mode shape to fit seamlessly into a quantum network.
Strategies such as controlled reversible inhomogeneous
broadening (CRIB) and atomic frequency combs (AFC)
have emerged to handle these processes, refining the
balance between efficiency, bandwidth, and operational
practicality.

No discussion of quantum memory is complete
without addressing coherence time and fidelity—two
metrics that quantify storage quality. Coherence time
measures how long a quantum state retains its defining
characteristics before environmental noise and internal
interactions induce degradation. Fidelity assesses the
accuracy with which the retrieved state matches the
original, a vital property for error-sensitive quantum
protocols. Extending coherence times is a perennial
challenge, as it requires shielding the memory from
magnetic fluctuations, temperature variations, and
other sources of noise. Techniques such as dynamic
decoupling sequences and isotopic purification of host
materials have pushed the boundaries, with some
systems now achieving coherence times long enough to
span classical communication delays over hundreds of
kilometers.

A defining ambition in quantum memory design is *on-
demand retrieval*, the controlled release of stored qubits
exactly when the network requires them. This capability
prevents bottlenecks and optimizes the temporal
coordination essential for entanglement swapping—the
fundamental operation in repeater chains. Achieving
on-demand access involves additional physical controls

such as dynamically tunable fields or switching mechanisms in the storage medium, enabling the conversion of stationary qubits back into photons at will. This is a substantial step beyond simple delay lines, embodying the dynamic flexibility that quantum networks demand.

Beyond storing single quantum bits, advanced memory architectures incorporate multiplexed storage. By storing multiple quantum states simultaneously—either segregating them spatially within different regions of the medium or temporally across consecutive time bins—multiplexing vastly increases the capacity and throughput of quantum channels. This is not merely a matter of volume; it reduces the latency and improves the rate at which entanglement can be established over long distances, essential for practical realizations of quantum internet architectures. Multiplexed quantum memories thus act like high-capacity buffers, smoothing the stochastic nature of photon arrivals inherent in quantum communication.

Effective integration with transmission channels represents another crucial layer of complexity. Quantum memories must be tailored to handle photons at the same wavelengths and bandwidths as those traveling through optical fibers or free space. For instance, many atomic memories naturally interact with visible or near-infrared light, while telecommunications infrastructure predominantly operates around 1550 nanometers due to minimal fiber loss. Bridging this spectral gap often requires frequency conversion interfaces or specially engineered media, ensuring that the stored photons can be efficiently coupled back into the communication network without sacrificing coherence or fidelity.

Yet, ambitions for large-scale quantum networks are

91

tempered by scalability challenges inherent in current
quantum memory technology.   Physical constraints
limit how densely memories can be packed while
maintaining isolation between stored qubits. Network-
level coordination imposes exacting synchronization
demands; as components multiply, so do opportunities
for temporal misalignment, noise accumulation, and
resource overheads.   Designing architectures that
balance complexity with reliability involves trade-offs
among memory capacity, coherence, and operational
speed—demands that push researchers toward hybrid
solutions and novel material platforms.

Ultimately, quantum memory stands as a linchpin in
the evolution of quantum communication. Its ability to
buffer, synchronize, and faithfully preserve quantum
information enables the deployment of repeaters and
networks that surpass the limits of direct transmission.
Advancements in materials science, control protocols,
and system integration steadily chip away at existing
barriers, bringing the vision of a robust, global quantum
internet closer to reality.   The next generation of
quantum networks will owe much to these silent
sentinels holding qubits in wait, ready to deploy them
precisely when and where they are needed.

Chapter 4

Key Quantum Communication Protocols

In this chapter, we examine the fundamental protocols that enable secure, high-fidelity quantum information transfer. Beginning with Quantum Key Distribution for provable secret sharing, we then detail Quantum Teleportation for state transfer via entanglement. Next, we explore Quantum Secret Sharing schemes that distribute information among multiple parties, before describing Entanglement Swapping methods at the heart of long-distance links. We conclude with strategies for Quantum Error Correction to protect against noise and techniques for Authenticated Encryption in the emerging quantum Internet.

4.1 Quantum Key Distribution (QKD)

Quantum Key Distribution (QKD) is a remarkable application of quantum mechanics that allows two distant parties to establish a secret cryptographic key with security guaranteed by the fundamental laws of physics. Unlike classical key exchange methods, which rely on mathematical complexity to fend off eavesdroppers, QKD offers provable security rooted in the very nature of quantum states. This quantum advantage arises primarily from two key principles: the *no-cloning theorem* and the inherent *disturbance caused by measurement*.

At its heart, the no-cloning theorem states that an unknown quantum state cannot be duplicated perfectly. Imagine trying to copy a quantum particle's state without altering it—nature forbids this. Consequently, if an eavesdropper attempts to intercept and replicate the quantum signals exchanged during key distribution, their intrusion necessarily introduces errors. Furthermore, any measurement on a quantum system irreversibly influences the state, ensuring that tampering is not only detectable but also leaves a trace visible to the communicating parties. These twin properties underpin the security of QKD and make undetected eavesdropping impossible in principle.

One of the earliest and most influential proposals to realize this idea is the *BB84 protocol*, introduced by Charles Bennett and Gilles Brassard in 1984. Although simple in concept, BB84 beautifully exploits quantum states and measurement to provide secure key generation. The protocol unfolds in several clearly defined steps.

First, the sender—commonly called Alice—prepares a sequence of quantum bits (qubits), each encoded in the polarization state of a photon. Each photon can carry a bit value, either 0 or 1, encoded in one of two possible *bases*: the rectilinear basis and the diagonal basis. The rectilinear basis encodes bits as horizontal ($\rightarrow$) or vertical ($\uparrow$) polarization, while the diagonal basis uses polarizations tilted at 45° ($\nearrow$) or 135° ($\nwarrow$). Choosing the basis randomly for each photon ensures that an eavesdropper cannot predict how the bits are encoded.

Once prepared, Alice sends these photons over a quantum channel—typically an optical fiber or free space—to the receiver, Bob. Bob, unaware of Alice's basis choices, measures each incoming photon in a randomly chosen basis (rectilinear or diagonal). Due to the quantum measurement postulate, Bob's measurement will yield a meaningful bit value only if his basis matches Alice's; otherwise, the outcome is probabilistic and yields no reliable information about Alice's original state.

Following the transmission and measurement phase comes the essential process of *basis reconciliation*. Using a classical public channel, Alice and Bob compare which bases they used, without revealing the actual bit values. They discard all bits where their bases did not match, retaining only those measured in the same basis—this is called *sifting*. The sifted key now comprises bits that have a high likelihood of matching perfectly, forming the raw key material for further processing.

However, real-world conditions and potential eavesdropping introduce errors, so Alice and Bob next estimate the *Quantum Bit Error Rate* (QBER) by comparing a subset of their raw key bits. If the QBER exceeds a certain threshold, they suspect eavesdropping or excessive noise and abort the protocol. Otherwise, the key is deemed sufficiently secure to proceed with *information reconciliation*.

Information reconciliation is a classical error-correction process designed to align Alice's and Bob's raw keys perfectly. Techniques such as the Cascade protocol involve iterative parity checks and error correction over the public channel, exposing minimal information to any adversary. This step ensures both parties hold identical keys despite transmission errors.

Yet, even after reconciliation, the key may not be fully secure. The partial information that might have leaked to an eavesdropper must be addressed. *Privacy amplification* is the final quantum cryptographic ingredient. By applying carefully chosen hash functions—mathematical operations that compress the raw key unpredictably—Alice and Bob distill a shorter, final key that is provably secret. This procedure effectively removes any residual information an eavesdropper might have gained, ensuring the secret key's unconditional security.

Further refinements to the BB84 protocol, such as *decoy-state methods*, enhance robustness against sophisticated attacks. Since practical photon sources emit multiple photons occasionally, an eavesdropper might exploit these through *photon-number-splitting* attacks, intercepting parts of multiphoton pulses without detection. Decoy states cleverly involve sending photons with varying intensities randomly, allowing Alice and Bob to detect anomalies in detection statistics that betray such attacks and adjust their key rates accordingly.

The unconditional security of QKD, proven through rigorous theoretical work, stands as a cornerstone achievement. Security proofs demonstrate that no matter what quantum attack an eavesdropper employs—even the most general and powerful—it is impossible to gain meaningful information without inducing detectable disturbances. These proofs rely on entanglement theory, quantum error correction bounds, and the laws of quantum information theory. While the mathematics is involved, the conclusion is elegant: QKD's security is guaranteed by the physics of the quantum world itself, not by computational assumptions.

Practical implementations, however, face many real-world challenges. Detector efficiencies, dark counts (false detection events in the absence of photons), channel loss, and environmental noise introduce imperfections. Finite-key effects, where only limited numbers of photons can be sent, require careful statistical methods to reliably estimate QBER and security parameters. These factors constrain the achievable distances and key generation rates but have driven innovative engineering and theoretical improvements, continuously pushing QKD from the laboratory to network prototypes and field deployments.

By harnessing the peculiarities of quantum physics, QKD offers a powerful solution to one of cryptography's fundamental problems: establishing secret keys securely in an untrusted environment. It transforms the elusive concept of trust into a physically testable condition, creating cryptographic keys whose secrecy is not just a hopeful assumption, but a scientifically guaranteed fact.

4.2 Quantum Teleportation

Quantum teleportation is one of the most captivating phenomena at the intersection of quantum mechanics and information theory. Unlike science fiction teleporters that physically transport objects instantaneously, quantum teleportation transmits the *state* of a quantum particle from one location to another without moving the particle itself. This seemingly magical feat relies on two key ingredients: shared entanglement between sender and receiver, and classical communication channels. Together, these allow the perfect transfer of an unknown quantum state, preserving all its subtle

97

quantum properties.

At its core, teleportation exploits the profound nonlocal correlations embedded in entangled states. Imagine Alice, the sender, holds a qubit in an arbitrary state $|\psi\rangle$ that she wants to transmit to Bob, the receiver. They share an entangled pair of qubits—one with Alice, one with Bob—prepared far in advance. Alice performs a special joint measurement on her unknown qubit and her half of the entangled pair, effectively "merging" the two and projecting them onto one of the four Bell states. This measurement scrambles her two qubits into one of four well-defined entangled outcomes, each corresponding to a unique pair of classical bits.

The magic is that Bob's distant qubit, untouched by any direct interaction, instantaneously assumes a state closely related to Alice's original qubit, but with a twist: it may be transformed by one of four possible quantum operations (known as Pauli corrections). To complete the teleportation, Alice sends Bob the two classical bits describing her measurement outcome. Upon receiving this information, Bob applies the appropriate local transformation to his qubit. The result? Bob's qubit now perfectly replicates the original state $|\psi\rangle$, as if the qubit itself teleported across space.

This protocol necessitates two critical resources. First is the entangled pair, which acts as a quantum bridge between Alice and Bob. One entangled pair per teleportation is required—not surprisingly, since entanglement acts as a fundamental currency in quantum information. Second is the classical communication channel, used to transmit the two bits of measurement outcome. Without this classical message, Bob's qubit remains in a superposition of all possible corrected states and cannot recover $|\psi\rangle$. Thus, teleportation ingeniously combines quantum and classical information flows to transfer quantum states.

A closer look at the key measurement reveals the central role of the *Bell-state measurement*. This is a joint measurement projecting onto the maximally entangled Bell basis, comprising four orthogonal states:

$$|B_{00}\rangle = \frac{|00\rangle + |11\rangle}{\sqrt{2}},$$
$$|B_{01}\rangle = \frac{|00\rangle - |11\rangle}{\sqrt{2}},$$
$$|B_{10}\rangle = \frac{|01\rangle + |10\rangle}{\sqrt{2}};$$
$$|B_{11}\rangle = \frac{|01\rangle - |10\rangle}{\sqrt{2}}.$$

By jointly measuring the unknown qubit and her entangled half in this basis, Alice disentangles her system while encoding the quantum state into Bob's qubit, up to a Pauli correlation dependent on the measurement outcome.

The interplay between quantum operations and classical communication means the overall state evolution can be expressed as:

$$|\psi\rangle_1 |\Phi^+\rangle_{23} = \frac{1}{2} \sum_{i,j=0}^{1} |B_{ij}\rangle_{12} (X^i Z^j) |\psi\rangle_3,$$

where $|\Phi^+\rangle$ is the shared entangled pair, and X, Z are the Pauli operators applied conditionally on the measurement bits i, j. This succinct expression embodies the entire teleportation circuit, where the initially unknown state $|\psi\rangle$ is reconstructed at particle 3 after applying the appropriate corrections.

Yet, teleportation does not guarantee perfection by itself. Real-world limitations arise from imperfect entanglement fidelity and measurement inaccuracies. Any deviation from a perfect maximally entangled state reduces teleportation fidelity—the degree to which Bob's reproduced state matches the original. Similarly, noise and errors in the Bell-state measurement introduce uncertainty, potentially scrambling the classical bits sent. Improving these factors remains at the frontier of experimental quantum information science, as the goal is to achieve fault-tolerant, high-fidelity teleportation suitable for scalable quantum networks.

A fundamental consequence of the protocol's design is the strict adherence to the *no-signaling principle*. Though Bob's qubit instantaneously changes upon Alice's measurement, he gains no usable information without the classical bits sent afterward. This ensures teleportation cannot transmit information faster than light, preserving causality and relativistic constraints.

Beyond the standard qubit teleportation, innovative variations extend the concept to continuous-variable systems, where information is encoded in properties like the quadratures of light fields, enabling teleportation of quantum states of light pulses. Multi-qubit teleportation schemes also exist, involving entangled states of higher dimension or multipartite correlations, paving the way for teleporting more complex quantum objects and entanglement itself.

Teleportation has moved from theoretical curiosity to practical reality in diverse physical platforms. Photonic experiments exploit the ease of generating and manipulating entangled photons, demonstrating long-distance quantum state transfer through optical fibers. Ion-trap systems use entanglement between ion qubits for teleportation within well-controlled atomic arrays, while superconducting circuits in the microwave regime enable solid-state implementations compatible with emerging quantum processors. Each platform faces unique technical challenges—such as photon loss, decoherence, or gate errors—but collectively they highlight teleportation's pivotal role in future quantum communication and distributed quantum computing architectures.

By allowing the faithful transmission of a quantum state without direct transmission of the encoded particle, teleportation revolutionizes our understanding of information transfer. It exemplifies how quantum mechanics permits new modes of communication rooted in entanglement and measurement—and promises to underpin the secure quantum networks, teleportation-based quantum repeaters, and ultimately the quantum internet of tomorrow.

4.3 Quantum Secret Sharing

In our journey through quantum information, we have seen how the fragile nature of quantum states both challenges and empowers new modes of communication and computation. Quantum secret sharing takes us deeper into the realm where secrets are not just classical bits locked away, but delicate quantum states distributed among several parties so that only authorized groups can reconstruct the secret. This concept blends the foundational mystery of quantum entanglement with the pragmatic need for secure and reliable multiparty cooperation.

- Imagine a scenario in which a sensitive quantum key or quantum-encoded data must be entrusted to a network of collaborators: no single individual holds the full secret, yet subsets of them can pool their pieces to recover it. This is the essence of *quan-*

101

tum secret sharing, a task crucial for secure multi-party computation where parties jointly perform a computation without revealing their private inputs, or for distributed quantum control where operational decisions depend on collective authorization. For example, financial institutions could distribute quantum secrets among branches so that only a quorum of branches can unlock sensitive information, adding layers of security that classical means cannot offer. The quantum nature of the data ensures heightened protection, exploiting phenomena inaccessible to classical cryptography.

The backbone of quantum secret sharing schemes is the (k, n) threshold structure: there are n parties, and any subset of k or more can reconstruct the secret, but subsets smaller than k remain completely ignorant of it. This threshold controls access and enforces collaboration. Unlike classical threshold schemes, quantum secret sharing must grapple with no-cloning—quantum states cannot be copied arbitrarily—adding a subtle but profound twist to how these shares are crafted and combined.

At its core, a (k, n) quantum scheme divides the secret quantum state into entangled shares, distributing them to n participants. The cleverness lies in embedding the secret such that only when at least k parties bring their shares together via a collective operation can the original state be faithfully reconstructed. Those with fewer shares face a puzzle with missing pieces, obtaining no useful quantum information.

One of the most elegant methods to realize such distribution uses the Greenberger–Horne–Zeilinger (GHZ) states, a form of multipartite entanglement involving three or more qubits. The GHZ state generalized to n parties takes the form:

$$\frac{1}{\sqrt{2}} \left(|0\rangle^{\otimes n} + |1\rangle^{\otimes n} \right),$$

a delicate superposition where all qubits collectively share coherence. This entanglement is the canvas on which the secret is painted. By encoding the secret qubit into this n-qubit GHZ backbone, we create correlations so tight that only when a sufficient number of parties cooperate does the original quantum information emerge.

The power of GHZ-state encoding stems from its collective parity and phase relationships. Each participant holds a share—a qubit from the entangled state—that by itself reveals no information. The GHZ state weaves these pieces into a tapestry where knowledge is inherently a group achievement.

Preparation begins with the dealer generating the entangled GHZ state, embedding the secret quantum information via unitary operations that correlate the secret with the entangled system. Once prepared, each participant receives one qubit of the GHZ state as their share. The physical distribution demands fragile care: entangled qubits must be transmitted with minimal decoherence over quantum channels to preserve coherence.

This sharing procedure ensures that the quantum information is never localized but rather inherently nonlocal, spread across the network. The dealer's role is akin to an orchestra conductor, who sets the entangled stage and hands out parts so that the players must unite their efforts to perform the symphony of recovery.

When an authorized subset of k or more parties decides to recover the secret, they convene to perform a collective quantum operation. This may involve applying joint unitary gates or coordinated measurements that

103

collapse their joint shares into the desired secret state. Crucially, these operations exploit the entanglement structure to extract the encoded quantum information with high fidelity.

For example, in a simple three-party GHZ scheme with a $(2, 3)$ threshold, any two participants can collaborate by performing appropriate local measurements followed by classical communication to reconstruct the secret qubit on one participant's system. The process mirrors classical secret collaboration but operates in the quantum realm, leveraging shared entanglement and careful measurement choices that avoid disturbing the fragile state prematurely.

One of the powerful guarantees of quantum secret sharing is security against collusion: groups smaller than the threshold k learn nothing about the secret, even if they pool their shares and perform any quantum operation allowed by physics. This security arises from the laws of quantum mechanics themselves rather than assumptions about computational hardness.

This unconditional security contrasts with classical schemes, reminding us how quantum states' nonlocal correlations can enforce strict access control. The no-cloning theorem ensures these unauthorized subsets cannot replicate missing shares. Their partial knowledge is essentially a maximally mixed state, devoid of clues about the original secret—a fortress built into the very fabric of quantum information.

Real quantum systems are imperfect. Qubits suffer decoherence, noise, and loss during preparation and distribution, risking the integrity of the secret. To tackle these realities, quantum secret sharing schemes often integrate quantum error correction techniques.

Error-correcting codes can encode a quantum secret

across redundant entangled shares so that even if some shares degrade or are lost, the secret can still be recovered accurately by the threshold group. For instance, stabilizer codes generalize the GHZ state into more robust constructs, building resilience against the practical imperfections of quantum hardware. This synergy between secret sharing and error correction is crucial for real-world applications where fidelity matters as much as security.

While early quantum secret sharing focused on qubits—two-level systems like spins or photons—modern research explores continuous variable (CV) systems, such as modes of light fields described by continuous spectra of position and momentum. CV quantum secret sharing encodes secrets into bosonic modes, leveraging squeezed states and Gaussian operations.

These continuous variable schemes naturally integrate with existing optical communication infrastructure, promising scalable and practical deployments. They adopt CV analogues of GHZ-type entangled resource states and reconstruct secrets via homodyne measurements and feedforward controls, expanding the versatility of quantum secret sharing to a broader physical domain.

Despite its elegance, quantum secret sharing confronts significant practical hurdles. Preparing high-fidelity, multipartite entangled states like large GHZ states remains experimentally demanding. The number of qubits involved quickly multiplies resource requirements: photon losses, imperfect gates, and decoherence threaten the integrity of shares.

Moreover, securely distributing entangled qubits over realistic quantum channels calls for error mitigation and robust verification protocols. Meeting stringent fidelity thresholds is pivotal, as small deviations can compromise both recoverability and security. Advances in quantum memories, photonic interfaces, and error correction bolster these efforts, but quantum secret sharing's leap from laboratory demonstrations to widespread deployment continues to challenge experimentalists and engineers alike.

Quantum secret sharing transforms the classical notion of distributed secrets into the quantum domain, exploiting entanglement to encode quantum information across multiple parties with precise threshold access control. By entwining secrets with GHZ states and their extensions, it ensures that collaboration is the key to recovery, while smaller coalitions remain blind to the secrets they covet. Its promise for secure multiparty quantum computation and distributed control foreshadows crucial roles in future quantum networks, even as practical realization navigates the challenging terrain of quantum coherence, noise, and engineering complexity. In this way, quantum secret sharing stands as a testament to the subtle power of quantum correlations to enforce trust and security beyond classical limits.

4.4 Entanglement Swapping

Entanglement—once thought of as a mysterious connection limited to pairs formed through direct interaction—can be extended across vast distances by harnessing a remarkable quantum trick known as *entanglement swapping*. Imagine two pairs of entangled qubits: one linking particles 1 and 2, the other linking particles 3 and 4. Although particles 1 and 4 have never directly interacted, a carefully orchestrated measurement on the intermediary particles 2 and 3 can conspire to entangle these distant qubits, effectively *swapping* the entanglement from the neighboring pairs to a new, remote pair. This process underlies one of the most elegant mechanisms for building quantum networks, connecting qubits separated by great distances without ever sending the entangled particles themselves the whole way.

The heart of entanglement swapping lies in performing a *Bell-state measurement* on the intermediate qubits (2 and 3). Such a measurement projects these two qubits jointly onto one of the four maximally entangled Bell states. This act collapses the state of the system in such a way that qubits 1 and 4 become entangled *conditioned on the outcome* of this measurement. The surprising twist is that before the measurement, qubits 1 and 4 were completely independent; no entanglement existed between them. But by measuring their partners in a special, entangled basis, the "spooky action at a distance" is redirected, enabling the creation of a fresh entangled link across regions that did not previously share quantum correlations.

To understand the concrete sequence behind entanglement swapping, consider the following steps. Initially, two entangled pairs are prepared: qubits 1 and 2 share a maximally entangled Bell state, as do qubits 3 and 4, each pair distributed across separate locations. Next, qubits 2 and 3 are brought together and subjected to a Bell measurement. The outcome of this measurement, which can be one of four possible Bell states, is then communicated via classical channels to the locations of qubits 1 and 4. Using this information, local corrective operations (such as specific quantum gates) are applied to either or both of these qubits. These corrections ensure that the resulting pair 1 and 4 is in a known, standard entangled state—typically the canonical $|\Phi^+\rangle$ Bell state. This sequence transforms two distinct entangled pairs into a single entangled pair that bridges previously unconnected nodes.

Mathematically, the initial state of two pairs in the $|\Phi^+\rangle$ Bell state can be expressed as:

$$|\Phi^+\rangle_{12} \otimes |\Phi^+\rangle_{34} = \frac{1}{2} \sum_{k=1}^{4} |\Psi_k\rangle_{23} \otimes |\Psi_k\rangle_{14},$$

where $|\Psi_k\rangle$ represent the four Bell states. After projecting qubits 2 and 3 onto a particular Bell state $|\Psi_m\rangle_{23}$, the corresponding qubits 1 and 4 are instantaneously projected into the matching Bell state $|\Psi_m\rangle_{14}$, up to local operations determined by the measurement result. This formalism reveals that measuring the middle link neatly transfers, or "swaps," the entanglement to the distant ends.

While elegant in principle, practical entanglement swapping must grapple with real-world imperfections. The success probability of the swap depends critically on detector efficiencies and channel losses. Imperfect detectors may fail to register the Bell measurement outcome or introduce errors, while photon losses in communication channels reduce the signal strength and thus the chance of successful entanglement distribution. Typical experiments achieve success probabilities well below unity, especially when involving photons traveling through fiber optic cables or free space. These inefficiencies mean that swapping must often be repeated multiple times or combined with error correction strategies to build reliable long-distance quantum links.

Entanglement swapping is the foundational building block for advanced quantum communication architectures known as *quantum repeaters*. Direct transmission of entangled states over long distances is severely limited by photon loss and noise; simply waiting for entanglement to survive the entire channel

108

is impractical. Instead, quantum repeaters divide the communication distance into shorter segments, create entangled pairs within each segment, and then use swapping at intermediate nodes to stitch these segments together. By concatenating swapping operations along a chain, entanglement can be extended across arbitrarily long distances in a scalable fashion. This hierarchical approach overcomes the exponential decay faced by direct transmission alone.

To keep communication time manageable and to maximize entanglement distribution rates, *nested entanglement swapping* techniques have been devised. These involve organizing swapping operations in multiple layers—starting with the shortest segments, then combining those into longer segments, and repeating this process up a hierarchy. Such nested schemes reduce latency by enabling parallel operations at different levels, dramatically improving scalability. They also open the door to sophisticated error management, allowing entanglement purification protocols to be interleaved with swapping steps, preserving higher-quality connections as the network grows.

Entanglement swapping can be implemented in two flavors: *heralded* and *deterministic*. Heralded swapping registers success only when the Bell measurement outcome is positively identified, effectively announcing that entanglement has been generated. This probabilistic scheme is simpler experimentally but requires repeated attempts before a successful swap is heralded. Deterministic swapping, on the other hand, guarantees the operation every time, often by exploiting strong interactions in matter-based systems or by engineering quantum gates that perform swapping on demand. While deterministic

109

implementations improve operational speed and reduce repetition, they are typically more challenging to realize with current technology, especially over long distances.

One persistent challenge in entanglement swapping is the preservation of *fidelity*—the quality or purity of the entangled state—as it undergoes successive swaps. Each swapping step introduces subtle imperfections and is exposed to environmental noise and decoherence, gradually degrading the strength of quantum correlations. Without careful error correction and purification, this cumulative degradation limits the distance and reliability of entanglement distribution. Managing fidelity loss thus remains at the forefront of quantum network design, balancing the complexity of hardware and protocols with achievable performance.

The versatility of entanglement swapping has inspired a diverse range of experimental platforms. Photons, with their low interaction with the environment and ease of transmission through optical fibers, are natural candidates and have been the workhorse for many optical demonstrations. Atomic ensembles and trapped ions, with their longer coherence times and strong interactions, provide excellent quantum memories suitable for deterministic swapping. Solid-state systems, such as nitrogen-vacancy centers in diamond and semiconductor quantum dots, exploit integrated fabrication and scalable architectures, merging photonic communication with matter-based processing. Each platform offers unique advantages and trade-offs, and hybrid approaches combining different systems aim to harness the best of all worlds.

Through entanglement swapping, what once seemed an insurmountable barrier in quantum communication— the direct entanglement of widely separated qubits without a shared past—has become a practical reality.

This protocol underpins the dream of a *quantum internet*, in which quantum information can be transmitted securely and instantaneously over global distances. The elegance of linking distant qubits by cleverly measuring their neighbors captures the essence of quantum mechanics: where observation not only probes reality but also actively creates new connections. By building on swapping, quantum networks are poised to revolutionize communication, computation, and our fundamental understanding of the quantum world.

4.5 Error Correction in Quantum Networks

Quantum networks, promising unparalleled capabilities in secure communication and distributed quantum computing, face a formidable adversary: errors. Unlike classical bits, quantum bits—*qubits*—are notoriously fragile, susceptible to a variety of disturbances arising from imperfect devices, noisy channels, and environmental interactions. Protecting delicate quantum information from such noise and operational imperfections is the linchpin that will determine whether quantum networking moves from laboratory curiosity to transformative technology.

Fundamentally, errors in quantum networks emerge when qubits, whether in transmission or storage, interact uncontrollably with their environment. Photons traversing optical fibers can undergo absorption or scattering; trapped ions used as memory qubits suffer from fluctuating electromagnetic fields; superconducting circuits suffer from thermal fluctuations and imprecise control pulses. These interactions cause *decoherence*, a process that erodes the quantum superpositions and entanglements that underpin quantum advantages. Additionally, gate operations themselves are imperfect, introducing systematic errors even before the qubits face the noisy channel. Combined, these effects make quantum data fleeting unless actively protected.

Classical error correction often relies on simple redundancy—copy a bit multiple times and perform majority voting to retrieve the original message. However, quantum states cannot be naively copied due to the no-cloning theorem, a fundamental restriction forbidding the creation of identical copies of unknown quantum states. This dilemma sparked the development of *quantum error-correction codes* (QECCs), ingenious schemes that encode a single *logical qubit* into an entangled state of several physical qubits. Instead of copying, quantum error correction spreads the information across a larger Hilbert space, so that damage to a few physical qubits can be diagnosed and corrected without ever directly measuring—and thus disturbing—the logical qubit's delicate superposition.

At the core of these codes is the notion of *logical qubits*: carefully constructed states representing the original quantum information, protected by a redundancy not of simple duplication but of entanglement and correlation. For instance, one of the earliest and simplest codes encodes a single logical qubit into three physical qubits, protecting against single bit-flip errors. Explicitly, the logical states are given by

$$|0_L\rangle = |000\rangle, \quad |1_L\rangle = |111\rangle,$$

where $|0_L\rangle$ and $|1_L\rangle$ denote the logical zero and one states respectively. If a single qubit flips erroneously, say the first qubit flips from 0 to 1, the resulting state might be $|100\rangle$. Although this is no longer equal to either logical basis state, the error can be detected by checking the parity between physical qubits, allowing a correction to restore the original logical qubit without ever measuring it directly.

Detecting which specific error occurred, however, requires a more subtle strategy than just comparison. Measuring the qubits directly would collapse their superposition, destroying the stored quantum information. The solution comes in the form of *stabilizer formalism*, a framework introduced to systematically identify errors without compromising the quantum data. Stabilizers are operators that leave the encoded logical states unchanged (i.e., the logical states are eigenstates with eigenvalue $+1$). When an error acts on the system, it changes the eigenvalues of certain stabilizers to -1. By repeatedly measuring these stabilizer operators—using ancillary qubits and cleverly designed circuits—one can extract an *error syndrome*, pinpointing which error has struck, and apply the correct recovery operation. The beauty is that these measurements do not reveal the quantum information itself but only the presence and type of errors.

Beyond these early codes, the field blossomed with the discovery of *topological codes*, which encode quantum information in global features of a lattice of qubits. Among these, *surface codes* have emerged as frontrunners due to their remarkable robustness and compatibility with physically local operations. Surface codes arrange qubits on a two-dimensional lattice where stabilizers form plaquettes preserving collective properties. Errors manifest as local defects that can be detected and corrected by measuring stabilizers around these plaquettes. Their topology makes it exponentially unlikely for errors to conspire and corrupt the logical qubit, granting surface codes higher *error thresholds*—the maximum physical qubit error rate below which quantum error correction can reliably improve fidelity. The practical advantage is that surface codes require only nearest-neighbor interactions and straightforward syndrome extraction, bringing large-scale fault-tolerant quantum networks within reach closer than once imagined.

Error correction alone does not guarantee reliable quantum networking; the *operations* used during communication and computation must also be designed to prevent the proliferation of errors. This motivation inspired the principles of *fault tolerance*, ensuring that an error in one part of the system does not cascade uncontrollably and corrupt other qubits or logical operations. Fault-tolerant protocols carefully design gates, state preparations, measurements, and error detection circuits to confine errors and correct them promptly. For example, certain gate constructions use transversal operations—applying the same physical gate to each qubit independently—preventing a single physical fault from spreading across the entire logical qubit. By meticulously combining fault tolerance with quantum error correction, quantum networks can in principle perform indefinitely long communication, computations, and storage.

Critically, the effectiveness of these techniques depends on achieving physical error rates below well-defined *error thresholds*. Experimental realizations to date suggest that modern quantum devices, while improving rapidly, must continue shrinking their operational error rates to the order of 10^{-3} to 10^{-4} or less, a steep but achievable target. Crossing this threshold flips the balance—from error accumulation dominating network fidelity to error correction suppressing noise sufficiently. Without this milestone, the overheads of error correction outweigh its benefits, leaving quantum states fragile and transient.

Speaking of overheads, quantum error correction comes with a notable price. Encoding a single logical qubit may require dozens, hundreds, or even thousands of physical qubits, depending on desired fidelity and error rates. Additionally, error correction protocols involve numerous ancillary qubits and repeated rounds of syndrome measurement—a complex choreography of gates and classical processing. This *resource overhead* includes not only qubit count but also increased circuit depth, longer memory times, and intricate control electronics. Balancing these trade-offs is an active research frontier, as practical quantum networks will have to optimize between achievable fidelity, system complexity, and operational cost.

Despite these challenges, error correction is seamlessly integrated into essential quantum network protocols. Take *quantum key distribution* (QKD), where secure cryptographic keys are exchanged using quantum states. Embedding error correction improves the reliability and distances over which secure keys can be generated. Similarly, *quantum teleportation* protocols—which transfer unknown quantum states via entanglement and classical communication—benefit from error-corrected entanglement links to prevent degradation. Most crucially, *quantum repeaters*, devices that extend communication distances by segmenting channels and performing entanglement swapping, rely heavily on error-correcting codes to purify and store entangled states, overcoming photon loss and noise intrinsic to optical fiber networks.

In sum, maintaining high-fidelity quantum information across networks involves a sophisticated interplay of encoding fragile quantum data into larger, redundant physical systems; diagnosing and correcting errors without collapsing the information;

115

and crafting fault-tolerant operations that constrain error propagation. Success hinges on surpassing error thresholds, managing resource overheads, and embedding these techniques deeply within quantum communication protocols. These strategies collectively form the backbone of practical quantum networking, transforming a once ephemeral quantum state into a resilient thread weaving together future quantum technologies.

4.6 Authenticated Encryption in the Quantum Age

Quantum communication promises unprecedented levels of security by harnessing the laws of physics rather than relying solely on mathematical complexity. However, the leap from confidential to authenticated encryption in the quantum setting is far from trivial. While quantum channels offer a fundamentally new kind of security, they do not eliminate the critical need for authentication, especially when classical data accompanies quantum transmissions. Ensuring both confidentiality and authenticity—two pillars of secure communication—remains vital as quantum networks move from theory to practice.

At first glance, quantum key distribution (QKD) might appear to provide perfect secrecy, thanks to its ability to detect eavesdropping and generate shared secret keys without exposing key material. Yet, quantum channels themselves must be overseen by classical control protocols: logins, handshakes, session initiations, and error corrections all travel as classical bits. These classical messages, if unauthenticated, become a weak link vulnerable to manipulation by adversaries. Without authentication, attackers can perform man-in-the-middle attacks, intercept or replay messages, or even impersonate legitimate parties to hijack the communication process. Therefore, authentication remains indispensable to safeguard the classical channels that orchestrate and complement quantum transmissions.

Integrating confidentiality into this framework typically relies heavily on keys generated by QKD. A distinguished approach to achieve information-theoretic confidentiality—a gold standard beyond computational assumptions—is the one-time pad (OTP). Here, keys derived from QKD serve as genuinely random, secret strings that XOR perfectly with the plaintext message. As long as the key is as long as the message and never reused, the ciphertext is mathematically unbreakable. While this method is elegant, it demands impeccable key management, including generating enough key material and coordinating its secure allocation during each communication session. The one-time pad's intrinsic simplicity meshes neatly with the quantum key material, forming the backbone of confidentiality in quantum-safe communication practices.

Authentication of classical messages accompanying quantum transmissions often employs message authentication codes (MACs). Traditional MACs depend on cryptographic hash functions, but to match the information-theoretic guarantees of QKD, universal hashing techniques—first introduced by Wegman and Carter—offer an elegant solution. Universal hashing constructs families of hash functions such that the probability of collisions between messages is minimal, even for an adversary with unlimited computing power. When combined with a secret key, these hashes produce authentication tags that verify the integrity and origin of a message. Importantly, Wegman–Carter MACs are composable with keys derived via QKD, facilitating unconditionally secure authentication that complements the confidentiality guaranteed by the one-time pad.

Beyond classical messages, quantum communication demands tools to secure the quantum states themselves. Quantum state authentication represents this frontier, where quantum states sent across noisy or adversarial channels are tagged and verified to detect tampering. Conceptually analogous to classical MACs but technically more subtle, these schemes apply quantum error-correcting codes combined with secret keys to encode states so that unauthorized modifications collapse the transmitted quantum information or introduce detectable errors. Such protocols not only defend against eavesdropping but also maintain the delicate quantum coherence required for subsequent quantum operations—critical in practical quantum networks and distributed quantum computing.

A cornerstone of modern cryptographic rigor is composable security: the assurance that protocols remain secure even when composed or layered within larger systems. In the quantum setting, this property is paramount. Individually secure components—QKD, OTP encryption, Wegman–Carter authentication—must integrate seamlessly without introducing vulnerabilities when used in concert. Composability ensures that the overall system's security does not degrade due to unforeseen interactions between its parts. For example, a quantum authentication scheme when combined with QKD-based encryption should not inadvertently leak information or open new attack vectors. Formal frameworks now exist to analyze and prove composable security in quantum protocols, giving practitioners confidence in deploying complex authenticated encryption systems on quantum networks.

One of the most insidious threats that authentication defeats is the man-in-the-middle attack, where an adversary intercepts, alters, or replays messages to confuse or control communicating parties. Even in quantum channels, where eavesdropping leads to detectable disturbances, an unauthenticated classical channel can be subverted in ways that allow an attacker to impersonate legitimate users. Properly designed authentication ensures that every message, classical or quantum, carries a cryptographic proof of origin and integrity. This proof prevents adversaries from injecting fake messages or replaying old communications, maintaining the protocol's freshness and trustworthiness. Without these protections, quantum networks risk falling prey to familiar yet pernicious attacks under a new guise.

Effective authenticated encryption in the quantum era also hinges on rigorous key management practices. Given that QKD-generated keys fuel both confidentiality (e.g., with OTP) and authentication tags (e.g., Wegman–Carter MACs), securing these keys against compromise is critical. Keys must have limited lifetimes to minimize exposure, be refreshed regularly to prevent reuse, and be stored in tamper-resistant environments. Even quantum-generated keys are vulnerable if subjected to poor operational hygiene. Best practices call for judicious policies governing key storage, access control, and lifecycle management, creating a disciplined framework that preserves the theoretical security benefits of quantum cryptography in real-world deployments.

Adding authentication layers introduces trade-offs in performance and resource consumption. For instance, generating and verifying authentication tags consumes computational power and can introduce latency, particularly in low-latency quantum networks designed for real-time communication. Additionally, consuming QKD keys for both encryption and authentication creates pressure on key generation rates and storage capacity, potentially limiting throughput or increasing operational costs. Balancing these factors involves thoughtful protocol design, leveraging efficient algorithms and hardware acceleration where possible, and understanding the practical constraints of the intended application—whether it be secure voice communication, financial transactions, or critical infrastructure control.

As quantum networks develop from experimental testbeds into operational systems, international standards bodies and industry consortia are starting to codify best practices. Emerging guidelines address how to combine QKD with information-theoretic encryption, universal hashing for authentication, and quantum state verification to build robust, interoperable systems. These standards seek to harmonize terminology, establish security benchmarks, and clarify implementation requirements to foster broader adoption and trust. They also encourage rigorous security proofs, composability considerations, and testing protocols, ensuring that the quantum security promises materialize into reliable reality rather than remaining academic curiosities.

Striking a balance between confidentiality and authenticity in the quantum age demands more than just quantum channels. It requires an intricate dance of classical and quantum cryptographic techniques, meticulously managed keys, and thoughtful system integration. Protecting both the content and provenance of messages ensures that communication remains secure against evolving threats, whether classical or quantum-enabled. By weaving together one-time pads, universal hashing, quantum state authentication, and composable security frameworks, practitioners can build quantum networks that are not only secret but trustworthy—a true foundation for the next generation of secure communication.

Chapter 5

Quantum Cryptography and Security

This chapter examines how quantum mechanics transforms the security landscape of modern communications. We begin by exploring the information-theoretic guarantees inherent in quantum protocols and the fundamental limits imposed by quantum laws. Next, we survey practical attack vectors and hardware vulnerabilities unique to quantum systems, then pivot to classical post-quantum cryptography methods designed to resist quantum adversaries. Building on these foundations, we envision future integrated architectures that blend quantum and classical safeguards, detail authentication techniques tailored for quantum networks, and conclude with evolving privacy considerations in a quantum-enabled world.

5.1 Security Strengths of Quantum Networks

Quantum networks promise a level of security that transcends conventional cryptographic schemes, founded not on assumptions about an adversary's computational power, but rather on the immutable laws of physics. At the core of this promise lies *information-*

theoretic security, a guarantee of secrecy that holds regardless of technological advances or algorithmic breakthroughs. Unlike classical cryptography, which often relies on the presumed difficulty of certain mathematical problems (like factoring large numbers), quantum communication exploits fundamental quantum principles to secure information in a manner that is, in principle, unbreakable.

The principle of information-theoretic security means that even an adversary wielding unlimited computational resources cannot glean meaningful information about a secret key or message without detection. This unconditional security emerges from the very nature of quantum states, which encode information in ways that classical signals cannot replicate or intercept invisibly. Thus, quantum networks fundamentally shift the playing field from "computational hardness" to "physical impossibility," providing a robust defense against future technological uncertainties.

Among the cornerstones of quantum security is the *no-cloning theorem,* a uniquely quantum constraint stating that it is impossible to create an exact copy of an unknown quantum state. This may sound like a subtle quantum quirk, but its implications are far-reaching. In practical terms, it forbids an eavesdropper from making duplicate copies of the quantum signals traveling between legitimate users. Without the ability to clone, an interceptor must perform a measurement to gain information, invariably disturbing the quantum state in a detectable manner. This inexorable trade-off between knowledge and disturbance forms the backbone of eavesdropping detection.

How exactly does this detection work? Quantum protocols harness the principle that measuring a quantum system generally alters its state. When an eavesdropper attempts to intercept and measure quantum bits (qubits), the act of measurement introduces errors in the transmitted data. By carefully monitoring the error rates of the received quantum signals, legitimate users can infer the presence of an eavesdropper. If the observed disturbance exceeds a predefined threshold, the communication is aborted to prevent information leakage. This mechanism transforms interception from a silent threat into a self-revealing act.

The security of quantum protocols is encapsulated within a rigorous framework defined by key concepts such as *secrecy, completeness,* and *soundness. Secrecy* ensures that the key shared between parties remains unknown to any adversary; *completeness* guarantees that honest participants successfully establish a key when no interference occurs; and *soundness* means that if the protocol does not terminate successfully, any partial information leaked is negligible. These criteria formalize the intuitive goal of secure communication and provide a basis for mathematically proving the robustness of quantum cryptographic protocols.

Moreover, quantum security frameworks emphasize the importance of *composable security,* a stringent requirement that security guarantees persist when multiple quantum protocols are combined. In real-world settings, cryptographic systems rarely operate in isolation—they form parts of larger, complex networks and applications. Composable security ensures that even when integrated with other cryptographic tasks, the secrecy and integrity of the quantum protocols remain intact. This property reinforces quantum communication's viability as a foundation for secure infrastructure in a future quantum internet.

However, quantum security is not without its practical

constraints. One subtle yet crucial trade-off appears between the rate at which secure keys can be generated and the *quantum bit error rate* (QBER), the fraction of qubits detected with errors. Intuitively, higher error rates imply more eavesdropping or noise and require more intensive error correction and privacy amplification, thereby reducing the net number of secure key bits distilled. This trade-off is concisely captured by the bound

$$R \geq 1 - 2H(\text{QBER}),$$

where R represents the key generation rate and $H(\text{QBER})$ is the binary entropy function quantifying the uncertainty introduced by errors. As QBER increases, the entropy term grows, shrinking the achievable key rate. Practically, this means that quantum protocols operate best under low-error conditions and have a critical threshold beyond which secure key generation is impossible.

Aspect	Classical Cryptography	Quantum Cryptography
Security Basis	Computational hardness assumptions	Physical laws and quantum mechanics
Key Secrecy	Conditional on limiting adversary's power	Unconditional and information-theoretic
Eavesdropping Detection	Indirect, often impossible	Direct via measurement-induced disturbance
Key Distribution	Requires trusted couriers or public-key	Self-checking, no trusted courier needed
Resistance to Future Tech	Vulnerable to quantum computing	Future-proof by design

Table 5.1: Comparison of security features between classical and quantum cryptography.

Yet, quantum networks encounter practical limitations that nuance their theoretical strengths. Finite-size statistical effects mean that, in realistic sessions with limited quantum data, parameter estimates (like error rates) carry uncertainty, which must be carefully accounted for to prevent security loopholes. Technical imperfections such as detector inefficiencies and dark counts—false signals arising from detector noise—introduce errors and reduce overall fidelity. Additionally, optical losses in fiber channels or free-space links diminish the number of photons reaching the receiver, constraining communication distance and key generation rates. Addressing these imperfections requires both technological advances and sophisticated protocol designs, which often balance security, throughput, and operational feasibility.

Despite these challenges, the fundamental security strengths of quantum networks remain unparalleled. They offer a provable, physics-rooted foundation for cryptography that transcends the limitations of classical approaches, with built-in mechanisms to detect and thwart eavesdropping, and rigorous definitions ensuring robust guarantees in practical deployment. The inherent linkage between information gain and disturbance, formalized by the no-cloning theorem and quantum measurement principles, elevates quantum communication from a theoretical curiosity to a promising pillar of secure communication in the emerging quantum age.

Through this synergy of deep physical insight and ingenious protocol engineering, quantum networks stand poised to deliver secrecy beyond the classical horizon—an advance both profound and practical in the quest to protect information in an increasingly interconnected world.

5.2 Potential Quantum Threats

Despite the revolutionary promise of quantum communication to secure information beyond the reach of eavesdroppers, real-world implementations confront a sobering reality: no technology is impervious to attack. Quantum communication systems, while theoretically unbreakable under ideal conditions, rely fundamentally on physical devices—lasers, detectors, fibers—and these tangible components inevitably introduce vulnerabilities. Understanding these practical threats clarifies the frontier between idealized security and the nuanced balance of trust and skepticism that underpins modern cryptography.

One primary avenue of exploitation arises from *device side-channel attacks*. These attacks do not breach the quantum principles themselves; instead, they capitalize on unintended physical emissions leaking from quantum hardware. Just as early telegraph systems betrayed secret messages through faint electromagnetic hums, quantum devices produce subtle signatures— thermal fluctuations, timing patterns, or minute power variations—that an adversary might capture.   By carefully monitoring these emissions, an attacker gains clues about secret keys or internal settings without tampering with the quantum states directly.   Side-channel vulnerabilities underscore how the *realization* of quantum protocols can betray their theory, much like a whisper in a crowded room discloses a secret even if the words are cryptographically scrambled.

Closely related, *detector blinding* offers a striking example of turning quantum defenses against themselves. Quantum detectors are delicate light sensors, designed to identify single photons encoding secure information. However, attackers can flood these detectors with bright classical light, pushing them into a "linear mode" that behaves like a classical detector rather than a quantum one. In this blinded state, the attacker regains control over measurement outcomes by selectively triggering detector clicks, effectively bypassing the inherent randomness quantum measurements depend on. This subversion transforms the once-trustworthy black box into a puppet, illustrating how manipulating hardware operation modes can erode security from within.

Another subtle yet insidious strategy targets the very nature of photon sources: *photon-number-splitting* (PNS) attacks exploit imperfections in single-photon generation. Most practical devices emit weak laser pulses rather than perfect single photons, occasionally producing multi-photon bursts. An eavesdropper can siphon off one photon from such a burst, retaining a perfect copy of the quantum information without disturbing the remaining photons sent to the legitimate receiver. Because this maneuver leaves no detectable trace in the quantum channel's error rates, it stealthily undermines the secrecy of the shared key. The PNS attack starkly reveals how the nuances of photon statistics matter profoundly to overall security, and how practical limitations blur the lines of theoretical guarantees.

Beyond passive listening, adversaries may attempt active probing through *Trojan-horse strategies*. By injecting carefully modulated light into components such as modulators or phase shifters, an attacker hopes to glean information about the devices' internal configurations. Reflected light carries imprints of settings or keys, akin to peering through a keyhole by shining a flashlight into a locked room. The challenge lies in detecting such covert probes, as legitimate quantum communication links are not normally designed to monitor inbound light beyond the controlled quantum signals. Trojan-horse attacks, therefore, exploit overlooked "backdoors," revealing the intricate interplay between optical engineering and cryptographic protection.

Manipulating the transmission medium itself introduces yet another layer of vulnerability. *Channel manipulation* can involve altering loss characteristics, timing delays, or polarization states to create exploitable discrepancies. For instance, by introducing selective losses or varying timing profiles, an attacker might induce errors that appear natural or mask their eavesdropping activities. These subtle tamperings complicate the distinction between benign noise and malicious interference, demanding that quantum communication protocols include robust error thresholds and anomaly detection. Channel manipulation reminds us that the quantum channel is not a passive conduit but an active battleground where trust is hard-earned.

Not all threats seek to extract keys quietly; some aim to disrupt communication outright. *Denial-of-service (DoS) attacks* flood the quantum channel with noise or overwhelm devices with excessive signals, preventing the successful establishment of shared keys. This form of assault, while not compromising secrecy directly, damages availability—a core tenet of secure communication often overlooked in theoretical discussions. DoS attacks emphasize that practical security entails not only secrecy but also resilience and reliability against interference.

Recognizing these multifaceted risks has driven the development of *measurement-device-independent* (MDI) quantum protocols. By shifting the locus of trust away from detectors—frequently the most vulnerable hardware elements—these protocols allow users to establish secure keys even when measurement devices are untrusted or potentially compromised. MDI schemes cleverly harness entanglement swapping and joint measurements performed by an untrusted relay, essentially outsourcing the most attack-prone components while preserving security. This innovation bridges the gap between ideal security assumptions and practical device imperfections, exemplifying how theoretical insights shape resilient system design.

However, technology alone cannot guarantee protection; *device characterization* is paramount. Rigorous testing, calibration, and ongoing monitoring of hardware behavior are essential to identify and close hardware loopholes before they become exploitable. This meticulous vetting—covering emission spectra, timing jitter, detector linearity, and stray light reflections— informs both hardware manufacturers and protocol designers. Only through comprehensive understanding of device idiosyncrasies can vulnerabilities be mitigated effectively, affirming that security is as much an engineering discipline as a theoretical exercise.

The panorama of potential quantum threats underscores a crucial lesson: achieving secure quantum communication requires more than elegant mathematics or clever protocols. It demands a holistic view, embracing the imperfections and unintended behaviors of real devices and channels, adapting with vigilance to evolving adversarial strategies. While quantum mechanics provides a formidable shield, it is the interplay of physics, engineering, and cryptography that ultimately determines whether the shield holds firm or falters.

Looking ahead, the challenge lies in balancing theoretical security with practical implementation, continually refining both hardware and protocols. Through innovations like side-channel-resistant designs, MDI protocols,

131

and rigorous device audits, the quantum communication community moves closer to fulfilling the promise of secure communication in an uncertain world, where trust must be crafted as carefully as qubits themselves.

5.3 Post-Quantum Cryptography

As the quantum computing revolution looms on the horizon, it poses a fascinating challenge and an urgent call to rethink the very foundations of digital security. Classical cryptographic systems, which underpin everything from online banking to secure communications, largely rely on mathematical problems that are believed to be hard for conventional computers but would succumb easily under the sheer computational power of a sufficiently advanced quantum computer. Post-quantum cryptography (PQC) steps in as a defense strategy: it seeks to design classical cryptographic methods resilient against adversaries wielding quantum computers, ensuring security both now and in the unpredictable future.

Post-quantum cryptography comprises algorithms that remain secure against the most powerful quantum attacks we can currently envision. Unlike quantum cryptography, which leverages the principles of quantum mechanics to achieve security, PQC solutions run on standard computers but rely on mathematical problems believed to resist quantum assaults. Their primary objectives are twofold: first, to preserve confidentiality, integrity, and authenticity even if large-scale quantum computers emerge; second, to do so without requiring exotic quantum hardware. In essence, PQC aims to future-proof our digital cryptographic infrastructure by identifying hard problems beyond the reach of quantum algorithms such as Shor's, which famously breaks the robustness of widely used schemes like RSA and ECC (Elliptic Curve Cryptography).

Among the leading candidates in PQC, lattice-based cryptography stands out for its strong theoretical foundations and versatile applications. The central idea involves complex geometric structures called lattices—infinite grids of points in multi-dimensional space. The security of these schemes often rests on hard computational problems like the *Shortest Vector Problem* (SVP), which, despite decades of research, no known efficient algorithm (classical or quantum) can solve robustly at large scales.

Lattice problems offer a remarkable advantage: they provide building blocks for a wide range of cryptographic primitives, including encryption, signatures, and even advanced functionalities like fully homomorphic encryption. Practical schemes such as Learning With Errors (LWE) and Ring-LWE have demonstrated both promising security margins and reasonable performance, making them strong PQC contenders. Beyond their mathematical elegance, lattice constructions are relatively straightforward to implement and can resist both classical and quantum attacks, forming a cornerstone of post-quantum proposals.

Another fruitful avenue for PQC is code-based cryptography, which roots its security in the difficulty of decoding random linear error-correcting codes. Originally pioneered by Robert McEliece in 1978, code-based schemes encrypt messages by hiding them within seemingly corrupted codewords. The problem of efficiently correcting random errors without the private decoding key is widely regarded as intractable—even for quantum machines.

While McEliece's original scheme uses large keys that can be a logistical challenge, its robustness and decades-long track record against cryptanalysis have cemented it as a reliable candidate. Researchers continue to explore variants and hybrids that balance key size, security, and practicality better, but the underlying hard problem remains a steadfast pillar for post-quantum encryption.

Digital signatures provide authenticity and non-repudiation, and hash-based signature schemes offer a uniquely elegant approach within PQC. These schemes derive security solely from the collision resistance of cryptographic hash functions—a property well-studied and less vulnerable to quantum attacks compared to integer factorization or discrete logarithms.

Originally devised as one-time or few-time signature mechanisms, hash-based signatures like the Merkle Signature Scheme cleverly aggregate multiple one-time keys into a single, verifiable public key, enabling repeated use without compromising security. Although their signatures and keys tend to be larger than classical counterparts, ongoing improvements have enhanced their efficiency and brought them closer to practical adoption. Hash-based signatures represent a robust fallback where long-term security and minimal assumptions matter most.

Diverse mathematical landscapes also enrich the PQC toolkit. Multivariate cryptography relies on the difficulty of solving systems of nonlinear polynomial equations over finite fields—a problem known to be NP-hard in general, and resistant to quantum speedups to date. Various multivariate schemes offer relatively small key sizes and efficient operations, although security assessments remain an evolving challenge.

Isogeny-based cryptography, a more recent entrant,

harnesses the rich structure of elliptic curves and their relationships via isogenies—morphisms preserving group structure. The idea is that navigating the complex web of isogeny maps is computationally hard, a problem quantum algorithms have yet to crack efficiently. Isogeny-based schemes promise compact keys and intriguing cryptographic properties, including potential for secure key exchange and even quantum-resistant versions of classical protocols, but practical deployment still hinges on rigorous analysis and optimization.

Recognizing the profound impact of a quantum future, the U.S. National Institute of Standards and Technology (NIST) embarked on an open, transparent campaign to standardize post-quantum algorithms. Since 2016, dozens of submissions have undergone rigorous evaluation, spanning lattice-, code-, hash-, multivariate-, and isogeny-based approaches.

This multi-year process involves extensive cryptanalysis, implementation testing, and performance benchmarking under realistic scenarios. By the mid-2020s, NIST has announced a shortlist of finalists and alternates slated to become official standards, setting the stage for widespread adoption. NIST's effort underscores the pragmatic reality: transitioning global cryptographic infrastructure requires balancing security, efficiency, and usability in the face of uncertain timelines for quantum advancements.

Designing post-quantum algorithms is a remarkable exercise in trade-offs. Unlike classical schemes, where compact keys and rapid computations are often achievable simultaneously, PQC protocols must navigate a delicate balance. For example, lattice-based schemes generally offer reasonable speed but larger keys; code-based methods boast high security but impose heavy storage requirements; hash-based signatures guarantee sound security assumptions yet yield bulky signatures.

This tension influences decisions spanning hardware constraints, protocol integration, and user experience. System builders and vendors face the intricate task of evaluating security margins, potential attack vectors, and computational overheads, all while ensuring interoperability with legacy systems. Such trade-offs remind us that post-quantum cryptography is as much about engineering resilience as mathematical ingenuity.

While post-quantum cryptography safeguards classical channels with classical computations, another frontier—quantum key distribution (QKD)—directly exploits quantum physics to distribute keys securely. Combining these paradigms yields hybrid architectures that enhance security by layering defenses: quantum-generated keys complement resilient post-quantum algorithms, serving as a hedge against potential flaws or future breakthroughs.

Such hybrid schemes acknowledge the complex security landscape, where no single solution can guarantee absolute protection indefinitely. They also reflect practical realities; quantum channels remain limited in range and accessibility, whereas PQC can be deployed broadly over existing networks. Together, they paint a picture of complementary strategies, each addressing distinct vulnerabilities in our cryptographic ecosystem.

Transitioning to post-quantum cryptography goes beyond selecting secure algorithms; it demands careful orchestration. Legacy systems must coexist with new protocols, standards must evolve, and software and hardware have to be updated without disrupting established services. Migration strategies emphasize gradual integration, fallback mechanisms, and extensive testing to avoid unintended vulnerabilities.

Interoperability remains a major concern, as heterogeneous environments require seamless communication between classical, hybrid, and post-quantum systems. Organizations must weigh costs of new key sizes, computational demands, and compatibility issues, along with educating users and administrators. Ultimately, successful deployment will hinge on robust standards, community consensus, and sustained commitment.

Post-quantum cryptography represents the most promising avenue for securing digital communications against the transformational threat posed by quantum computers. Grounded in diverse mathematical problems believed to resist quantum attacks, PQC algorithms bring a rich spectrum of options—lattices, codes, hashes, multivariate polynomials, and isogenies— that collectively broaden the horizons of cryptographic design. The ongoing standardization efforts, along with practical considerations regarding performance and deployment, reflect a global endeavor to safeguard the information fabric of the future. Far from sidelining quantum cryptography, PQC complements it, crafting a layered, adaptive defense that anticipates threats yet remains rooted firmly in the classical computing world we navigate today.

5.4 The Future of Secure Communication

The landscape of secure communication is poised for a transformation as revolutionary as the advent of the internet itself. At its core, the future will be defined by a subtle yet powerful marriage of quantum and classical technologies, each complementing the other to build networks that are not only secure against today's threats, but resilient in the face of tomorrow's unknowns. This hybrid approach addresses critical limitations of existing infrastructures and promises a new era where privacy and trust are woven deeply into the very fabric of global connectivity.

- **Global QKD Infrastructures**

  Quantum key distribution (QKD) has long been celebrated as a breakthrough in secure communication, offering theoretically unbreakable cryptographic keys through the fundamental laws of quantum physics. Yet, early implementations often resembled isolated islands—single point-to-point links covering modest distances. The imminent challenge is to evolve these into continental-scale quantum backbones, capable of supporting a vast array of users and applications.

  Scaling QKD requires developing high-performance quantum repeaters and trusted-node architectures that maintain the integrity of the quantum keys over hundreds and even thousands of kilometers. Countries and consortia around the world are actively constructing city-to-city QKD networks, gradually knitting together regional webs that hint at the future quantum internet. These infrastructures do not seek to replace classical networks overnight; rather, they overlay specialized quantum channels on existing fiber-optic paths, enhancing security without disrupting familiar communication patterns.

  Moreover, such global infrastructures promote redundancies and route diversity, ensuring that even if one link is compromised or fails, secure communication can be dynamically rerouted. This vision aligns with the practical realities of deployment, where infrastructure must be robust, scalable, and economically feasible.

- **Satellite-Ground Integration**

    Covering the vast expanses between continents and remote regions remains a fundamental obstacle for purely fiber-based quantum links. Enter satellites—the eyes and ears in the sky that enable quantum signals to leap across oceans and rugged terrain without the attenuation that plagues ground-based channels.

    Hybrid architectures combining free-space quantum communication via satellites and terrestrial fiber networks are emerging as the blueprint for truly global coverage. Quantum payloads aboard low-Earth orbit satellites can exchange cryptographic keys with diverse ground stations scattered worldwide, effectively forming quantum "hubs" in the stratosphere. These hubs then connect into terrestrial QKD backbones, extending quantum security from dense urban centers to the farthest reaches of the planet.

    The feat is not trivial: free-space quantum communication faces challenges such as atmospheric turbulence, precise beam alignment, and limited contact windows. Nonetheless, recent successful demonstrations—such as distributing quantum keys between satellite Micius and ground stations thousands of kilometers apart— have proven the concept and energized investment worldwide.

- **Trust Models and Federations**

139

As networks grow both in scale and complexity, the question of trust—who controls keys, how they are managed, and to what extent parties rely on one another—becomes ever more pressing. Unlike classical cryptography that depends heavily on centralized authorities or public key infrastructures, quantum-enhanced networks invite novel frameworks for distributed trust.

Federations of independent domain operators emerge as a solution, enabling cross-domain key management that respects sovereignty but facilitates interoperability. In such federations, trust is delegated through transparent protocols and auditable mechanisms, ensuring that no single party wields unchecked power over the network's cryptographic backbone.

These models reflect a broader shift from hierarchical, monolithic security systems toward more democratic and resilient architectures. They also echo the decentralizing spirit found in other emerging technologies like blockchain, embedding trust not in opaque authorities but in collective agreements and verifiable operations.

- **Policy and Regulation**

    A technology as powerful and sensitive as quantum-secure communication cannot develop in a vacuum. Governments and international bodies are actively crafting the legal and regulatory scaffolding that will govern the use, export, and standards compliance of quantum cryptography devices and networks.

    These policies must balance national security imperatives, economic competitiveness, and privacy rights. Export controls, in particular, present thorny questions: ensuring that quantum communication technologies do not fall into adversarial hands while enabling legitimate international collaboration and commerce.

Additionally, regulatory clarity fosters innovation by providing firms and institutions with predictable frameworks for investment and deployment. The emergence of international standards for quantum key rates, interface protocols, and security certifications will serve as foundational benchmarks—much as the TLS protocols have shaped classical internet security over the past decades.

- **Adaptive Security Layers**

    Cyber adversaries do not stand still; their tactics evolve alongside new defenses. Next-generation secure communication networks therefore adopt adaptive security layers that can seamlessly integrate both quantum and post-quantum cryptographic protections in real time.

    In practice, this means quantum keys may be used to bootstrap classical encryption methods that have been hardened against quantum computational attacks, creating a layered defense that anticipates multiple threat vectors. Network nodes equipped with smart control systems can monitor the integrity of quantum channels and switch dynamically to alternative cryptographic algorithms or pathways if anomalies arise.

    Such adaptability transforms networks from fixed entities into living systems, capable of evolving their security postures in response to environmental signals and detected cyber threats. This fluidity is crucial in an era where the time lag between vulnerability discovery and exploitation can be measured in hours or minutes.

- **Interoperability Challenges**

  The promise of future quantum-enhanced networks hinges on their ability to merge smoothly with vast, heterogeneous legacy infrastructures. Achieving interoperability presents both technical and operational challenges, from protocol standardization to hardware compatibility.

  Legacy equipment, optimized for classical signals, must coexist with emerging quantum hardware without causing bottlenecks or security gaps. Protocol stacks need to be extended or redesigned to encapsulate quantum key exchanges alongside traditional encryption mechanisms. Network operators face the daunting task of upgrading and certifying components in a highly distributed ecosystem—often constrained by competing vendor architectures and budget limitations.

  Despite these challenges, incremental approaches have shown promise: implementing quantum-safe cryptography in tunnels over classical networks, developing middleware that abstracts quantum interfaces, and creating hybrid routers that intelligently mediate between classical and quantum data flows.

- **Roadmap and Milestones**

  The trajectory toward a quantum-secure communication future is marked by clear milestones, each representing a concrete step from theory toward broad deployment. Within the coming decade, expect to see widespread adoption of metropolitan QKD networks integrating thousands of users, expansion of satellite-based quantum key distribution from demonstration to commercial service, and initial federated trust consortia operating across national boundaries.

Standardization groups—including international telecommunication unions and cryptographic alliances—are scheduled to finalize foundational protocols and certification criteria. Concurrently, advances in quantum repeaters and error correction are expected to overcome current distance limitations, enabling long-haul quantum links without trusted nodes.

This roadmap balances optimism with pragmatism: robust infrastructure components will mature alongside policy frameworks and interoperability solutions. By the 2030s, quantum and classical security architectures will likely converge into cohesive, dynamic networks that are resilient in the face of evolving threats.

- **Open Research Directions**

  While much progress has been made, several frontier challenges await further exploration. Efficient quantum repeaters with low error rates and scalable designs remain a critical bottleneck. Likewise, protocols for dynamic trust delegation and federated key management are still in early theoretical and experimental stages.

  Hybrid security algorithms that optimally combine quantum and classical primitives require deeper mathematical and hardware insights. The human dimension—usability, device certification, and managing the complexity of hybrid cryptographic environments—must also be prioritized for real-world adoption.

Cross-disciplinary collaboration among physicists, computer scientists, cryptographers, and policymakers will accelerate breakthroughs. An open ecosystem encouraging experimentation, transparent benchmarking, and international cooperation is essential to navigating the complex socio-technical terrain ahead.

The future of secure communication is neither purely quantum nor solely classical but a sophisticated synthesis of both. Through scalable quantum key distribution networks spanning continents, seamless integration of satellite and terrestrial links, innovative trust federations, and adaptive security layers, next-generation infrastructures promise an unprecedented level of privacy and integrity. Navigating interoperability challenges, evolving regulatory landscapes, and a clear roadmap toward readiness, this vision is rapidly crystallizing. Yet, it remains an ambitious journey demanding continued innovation, vigilance, and global partnership to realize a truly quantum-secure world.

5.5 Quantum Authentication Protocols

As quantum communication technologies advance, securing the channel is only part of the story. Verifying that a message truly comes from the claimed sender and has not been altered—authentication—is equally critical. Although quantum channels offer unprecedented confidentiality, they do not automatically guarantee the integrity or origin of messages. Without robust authentication, adversaries can impersonate legitimate parties or tamper with data, undermining the promises of quantum security. The intricate dance of quantum states requires equally sophisticated methods to confirm not just secrecy, but trustworthiness.

At its core, authentication in quantum contexts must address message integrity and source verification over quantum links, where classical assumptions may no longer hold. Quantum protocols often generate shared keys or transmit quantum states themselves, but these processes remain vulnerable if an adversary hijacks the communication endpoint or injects false signals. Thus, modern quantum communication demands a layered security approach combining quantum and classical tools.

One well-known cornerstone in quantum cryptography is Quantum Key Distribution (QKD), which enables two parties to create shared, secret random keys. When these keys are employed with a one-time pad, a classical encryption technique where the key is as long as the message, communications achieve perfect confidentiality: no adversary can decrypt the message, even with infinite computational power. However, for perfect privacy to translate into real-world security, the legitimacy of the participants must be confirmed. An elegant synergy emerges by combining QKD with message authentication codes (MACs), ensuring that messages are both secret and genuine.

Classical cryptographic primitives continue to play an essential role alongside quantum protocols. In particular, the Wegman–Carter construction provides a lightweight and information-theoretically secure method for authenticating classical messages, such as control signals accompanying quantum transmissions. This approach uses families of universal hash functions in conjunction with secret keys, yielding MACs that resist forgery even against adversaries equipped with unlimited computing resources. By integrating Wegman–Carter schemes, quantum communication systems maintain the integrity of classical data exchanges, a vital prerequisite for error correction, reconciliation, and key distillation phases inherent in QKD setups.

The realm of digital signatures also extends naturally into the quantum domain, prompting the development of *quantum digital signatures* (QDS). Unlike classical digital signatures that rely on computational hardness assumptions, QDS protocols strive for unforgeability and verifiability derived from the laws of quantum physics. These schemes typically employ sequences of quantum states distributed among participants, enabling recipients to confirm origin authenticity while ensuring that no forgery or repudiation can occur. Quantum digital signatures are particularly promising for future networks where nonrepudiation—proof that a specific party did indeed send a message—remains a critical legal and transactional requirement.

Another fascinating avenue involves *quantum identity verification*, which leverages quantum states in challenge-response protocols to authenticate parties uniquely. Here, a verifier sends a quantum "challenge" state that only the legitimate claimant can correctly respond to, thanks to secret quantum information or specialized quantum processing abilities. Such protocols exploit quantum no-cloning and measurement disturbance properties, making them significantly harder to impersonate than classical counterparts. As quantum technologies mature, such identity verification mechanisms promise to enable secure access control and robust entity authentication without relying on passwords or classical secrets.

Ensuring that quantum data packets themselves have not been altered introduces the concept of *state authentication*. This involves "tagging" quantum states with auxiliary information designed to reveal tampering attempts. Protocols commonly employ quantum error-detecting codes combined with secret keys to embed authentication tags, allowing recipients to verify integrity upon reception. These techniques must delicately balance protecting fragile quantum states from noise while also detecting intentional interference, a challenge compounded by the fact that measurement generally disturbs quantum data. State authentication protocols thus represent a subtle art of preserving quantum coherence alongside integrity assurances.

Underlying these varied authentication mechanisms are rigorous *security proof frameworks* developed to guarantee that authentication remains reliable even under elaborate attack models and composability requirements. Such frameworks extend beyond demonstrating resilience against isolated attacks; they analyze how composed protocols maintain security when combined in complex quantum communication systems. By establishing formal mathematical models and security definitions, researchers ensure that authentication techniques do not become weak links in the broader quantum cryptographic chain, providing users with provable guarantees instead of mere assumptions.

Despite theoretical elegance, practical implementation of quantum authentication protocols confronts real-world constraints. Key consumption rates must be efficient enough to sustain high-throughput communication without exhausting limited secret keys. Latency—the delay introduced by authentication computations and classical communication—should remain minimal to preserve the overall performance of quantum networks. Moreover, the trustworthiness of physical devices themselves becomes pivotal, as hardware imperfections or side-channel vulnerabilities can undermine even the strongest theoretical protections. Striking the right balance between security, efficiency, and device assumptions remains an active area of experimental and engineering research.

Recognizing the importance of interoperability and standardization, international efforts are underway to establish *emerging standards* for quantum authentication protocols. Bodies such as the International Telecommunication Union (ITU) and national institutes are collaborating to define common formats, security criteria, and interfaces for authentication in quantum networks. These initiatives aim to bridge diverse quantum technologies, facilitate integration into existing infrastructures, and foster widespread adoption by providing clear guidelines for implementers and users alike. Standardized protocols will be essential to build scalable, economical, and universally trusted quantum communication systems.

The landscape of quantum authentication is thus a rich tapestry woven from quantum physics, classical cryptography, and practical engineering. Authenticating messages and verifying origins over quantum channels do not merely replicate classical security solutions; they transform them, adapting to the peculiarities and opportunities inherent in quantum information. By combining the unconditional secrecy of QKD with information-theoretically secure MACs, implementing quantum digital signatures, and employing sophisticated state authentication, future quantum networks can ensure messages remain inviolate, trustworthy, and accountable. As quantum technologies edge closer to mainstream deployment, robust authentication protocols will form the cornerstone of a secure quantum communication era, turning quantum's enigmatic potential into tangible, reliable trust.

5.6 Privacy in a Quantum World

The advent of quantum technologies promises transformative advances across communication, computation, and sensing. Yet, with these breakthroughs come novel challenges to one of the pillars of modern digital life: privacy. In a world powered by quantum-enabled networks, the traditional assumptions underpinning data confidentiality, anonymity, and control face fundamental reconsideration. Understanding this evolving landscape requires examining how quantum capabilities redefine both the threats to privacy and the tools for safeguarding it.

Quantum Privacy Threats

Quantum adversaries pose an unprecedented risk to data privacy due to their ability to harness quantum algorithms that can break many classical cryptographic protocols upon which current secure communications rely. Shor's algorithm, for example, can factor large numbers exponentially faster than classical methods, threatening traditional public-key cryptosystems like RSA and ECC. While this is a widely acknowledged risk, even more subtle forms of quantum-enabled data collection and inference amplify privacy concerns.

Quantum adversaries can covertly gather quantum-encrypted data streams, exploiting entanglement and measurement strategies to extract information that classical eavesdroppers could not access. Unlike

149

classical attackers who must observe bits, quantum adversaries target qubits, probing the delicate quantum states without necessarily collapsing them—at least not immediately. This enables a richer spectrum of inference attacks, where partial quantum information may be retained and processed later, possibly in combination with future technologies or side-channel data, thereby undermining long-term privacy guarantees.

Differential Privacy Adaptations

One classical approach to protecting data privacy in analytics is differential privacy, a framework that injects random noise into outputs to obscure the presence or absence of an individual's data. Extending these guarantees into the quantum domain has become a burgeoning research area. Quantum differential privacy adapts these principles to quantum data outputs, ensuring that measurements on quantum states reveal minimal information about any individual's contribution.

Such adaptations are nontrivial. Quantum data's probabilistic nature and the no-cloning theorem— meaning quantum information cannot be copied arbitrarily—impose constraints but also offer new levers of control. For example, mechanisms designed to add noise to the quantum measurement statistics can be carefully calibrated to balance utility with privacy. This quantum-tuned privacy accounts not only for classical leakage but also subtler quantum correlations that could otherwise betray sensitive information.

Anonymity Network Designs

Beyond secure data, anonymity itself must be rethought in quantum-enabled communications. Classic models such as mix-nets and onion routing, which shuffle and encrypt data across multiple nodes to conceal the source and destination, face new challenges when integrated with quantum links.

Quantum-compatible anonymity networks leverage principles like quantum key distribution (QKD) to secure each hop with provable security unmatched by classical keys. Moreover, the quantum no-cloning property restricts eavesdropping on routing paths, enhancing anonymity guarantees. Nevertheless, designing these networks demands novel architectures that preserve the classical anonymity properties while seamlessly interfacing with quantum channels. Such designs are vital for future quantum internet frameworks, where users expect not only confidentiality but also untraceability in their communications.

Secure Multiparty Quantum Computation

Collaborative data processing often pits privacy against utility: how to compute joint functions over private inputs without revealing those inputs themselves. Secure multiparty computation (SMC) addresses this classically, but quantum computing extends its scope and complexity.

Secure multiparty quantum computation allows participants to jointly perform quantum algorithms on their combined inputs while ensuring no one learns others' private data, beyond what can be inferred from the shared outputs. This paradigm exploits entanglement and quantum teleportation protocols, enabling complex computations that neither party could efficiently perform alone. In practical terms, secure quantum computation could, for example, empower consortia to analyze aggregated datasets—such as medical or financial records—with rigorous privacy assurances uncommon in current classical frameworks.

Blind Quantum Computing

Another intriguing privacy tool enabled by quantum mechanics is blind quantum computing. This approach envisions a client delegating computation tasks to a quantum server while keeping the nature of inputs, outputs, and even the algorithm itself completely private from the server.

By cleverly encoding the problem into quantum states whose exact form is hidden via quantum randomness and classical disguising, blind quantum computing ensures the server processes qubits without gleaning any meaningful information. This client-server model is especially relevant in the near-term quantum era, where access to powerful quantum hardware might be limited to cloud-based services. Users can thus harness quantum advantages without exposing sensitive data or proprietary algorithms, forging new avenues for privacy-preserving quantum cloud computation.

Data Minimization Principles

Even as quantum technologies augment data processing, foundational privacy principles remain crucial. Data minimization—the practice of limiting data collection and retention to the bare essentials—takes on renewed significance. Quantum systems, by their very nature, are difficult to clone or back up due to quantum no-cloning. This property can both aid privacy, by discouraging data replication, and challenge it, as lost quantum data may be irrecoverable without prudent management.

In quantum-enabled networks, minimizing quantum data footprints serves as a practical hedge against exposure, since any retained quantum information may be vulnerable to future breakthroughs in quantum attacks. Organizations must rethink data lifecycle policies, balancing the drive for quantum-enhanced analytics with strict controls on data retention and sharing, reducing the attack surface in this nascent environment.

Legal and Ethical Frameworks

Privacy in the quantum era is not solely a technical challenge but also a social and legal one. Existing regulations such as the European Union's General Data Protection Regulation (GDPR) codify rights for data control, transparency, and consent tailored to classical information systems. Quantum-enabled services prompt urgent discussions on how these frameworks translate or must evolve.

For instance, the immutable and highly sensitive nature of quantum data might require novel consent models or audit mechanisms. Questions arise about accountability when quantum algorithms—often probabilistic and complex—make decisions affecting individuals. Ethical considerations also emerge from the uneven global distribution of quantum capabilities, potentially exacerbating digital divides and surveillance imbalances. Regulators and ethicists must therefore collaborate closely with technologists to draft adaptable, inclusive policies that preserve foundational privacy rights in the face of quantum disruptions.

Privacy Standardization Efforts

Complementing legal evolution are technical standardization efforts, where international bodies and industry consortia strive to establish best practices and common protocols for privacy management in quantum applications. These initiatives address issues ranging from secure quantum key management to interoperability of quantum-enabled anonymity services, and from quantum differential privacy parameters to audit frameworks for blind computing.

153

Standards provide crucial benchmarks ensuring that privacy protections are not mere theoretical ideals but robust, verifiable realities across diverse quantum systems and vendors. By harmonizing terminology, metrics, and techniques, such efforts enable users to trust quantum services and encourage widespread adoption without compromising fundamental privacy guarantees.

Future Research Topics

The quantum privacy frontier bristles with compelling open questions. Among these are how to model privacy risks in hybrid classical-quantum systems, the limits of privacy amplification when quantum side information is available, and the potential for quantum machine learning algorithms to infer sensitive data from obfuscated inputs.

Moreover, embedding ethical considerations directly into quantum algorithm design—sometimes called "privacy by design"—remains an underexplored yet critical theme. The interplay between quantum communication complexity and privacy-preserving protocols invites innovation, as does the prospect of constructing quantum-resilient anonymous marketplaces and voting schemes. Continuous dialogue among quantum physicists, computer scientists, policymakers, and ethicists will be essential to navigate this evolving terrain thoughtfully.

Privacy in a New Paradigm

Privacy in a quantum-enabled world transcends mere extension of classical concepts, inviting a reimagination shaped by the unique properties of quantum information. While quantum computers pose new threats by breaking established cryptosystems, quantum mechanics also endows novel tools to protect and even enhance privacy. From quantum differential privacy to blind computing, the emerging suite of quantum privacy technologies promises richer, more nuanced protections attuned to a digital landscape increasingly interwoven with qubits.

At the same time, these opportunities must be tempered with careful governance, principled design, and proactive standard setting. The promise of quantum privacy depends not only on scientific ingenuity but also on cultivating public trust and embedding respect for individual rights at every layer. As quantum networks mature, they chart a path toward a future where privacy is not sacrificed on the altar of innovation, but rather redefined and strengthened through it.

Chapter 6

Programming the Quantum Internet

This chapter provides a hands-on guide to writing software for quantum networking applications. We begin with essential quantum computing concepts and the circuit model for programmers, then introduce key communication algorithms and how they translate into code. Next, we survey leading simulation frameworks and tools, before demonstrating practical code patterns for core quantum protocol routines. We then cover robust strategies for error handling and debugging in hybrid quantum-classical programs, and conclude by highlighting active open-source projects where readers can explore, contribute, and collaborate.

6.1   Quantum Computing Basics

At the heart of quantum computing lies the quantum circuit model, a beautifully elegant framework capable of harnessing the strange laws of quantum mechanics to perform computations beyond classical reach. To appreciate how this is realized in practice, we must first demystify the core abstractions and primitives that make quantum programs tick: qubits, quantum gates, measurement, and the scaffolding within which they operate. These concepts serve as the building blocks for quantum algorithms, and understanding them reveals why quantum computing is not merely faster classical computing but a fundamentally different endeavor.

The qubit, or quantum bit, is the quantum analog of the binary bit in classical computing. Yet unlike a classical bit, which is either 0 or 1, a qubit lives in a superposition—a continuum of states represented mathematically by complex vectors. In modern quantum programming languages, qubits are encapsulated as programmable objects that retain their quantum state internally and expose methods for manipulation and measurement. These abstractions allow programmers to treat qubits conceptually like registers in classical code, while the underlying system manages their delicate quantum nature.

Quantum programs seldom act on solitary qubits alone. More often, they manage *multi-qubit registers*—arrays or collections of qubits—from which one can execute batch operations, entangle qubits, or perform joint measurements. Grouping qubits this way parallels classical arrays but with richer interactions; since quantum states combine via tensor products, a register of n qubits inhabits a 2^n-dimensional state space. This exponentiation underpins the extraordinary computational power of quantum computers but also poses significant challenges for simulation and understanding.

To bridge the gap between abstract code and quantum theory, it helps to recall the mathematical representation of qubit states as *state vectors* in Dirac notation. Each qubit's state is denoted as $|\psi\rangle$, a vector in a two-dimensional complex Hilbert space. When programming, data structures holding qubit states correspond directly to these vectors or their higher-dimensional equivalents for multi-qubit registers. This direct mapping is not just elegant but essential for simulating quantum circuits on classical machines and verifying correctness.

Manipulating qubit states is achieved through *quantum gates*, the quantum counterpart of classical logic gates. Single-qubit gates are represented by unitary matrices applied to the qubit's state vector, rotating and changing its amplitude without collapsing the superposition. Familiar foundational gates include the Pauli-X (bit-flip), Hadamard (creating equal superpositions), and phase-shift operations. For illustration, consider the matrices for the X and H gates:

$$X = \begin{pmatrix} 0 & 1 \\ 1 & 0 \end{pmatrix}, \quad H = \frac{1}{\sqrt{2}} \begin{pmatrix} 1 & 1 \\ 1 & -1 \end{pmatrix}.$$

These operators elegantly encapsulate quantum transformations that a programmer invokes programmatically—applying a Hadamard gate to a qubit initialized in state $|0\rangle$ creates a balanced superposition $\frac{1}{\sqrt{2}}(|0\rangle + |1\rangle)$, the cornerstone of many quantum algorithms.

Beyond single-qubit manipulations, quantum power often emerges from *controlled gates* that operate conditionally based on the state of a control qubit. The canonical example is the controlled-NOT, or CNOT gate, which flips the target qubit if and only if the control qubit is in $|1\rangle$. Such two-qubit gates are the essential ingredients for creating *entanglement*, a uniquely quantum correlation with no classical counterpart. Coding these gates requires specifying control-target pairs, enabling conditional operations fundamental to quantum logic.

Quantum circuits themselves are sequences of such gates arranged in time order. Modern quantum programming environments offer *circuit construction APIs*—toolkits designed to compose, manipulate, and optimize these sequences as executable entities. Programmers build circuits incrementally by adding

159

gates to qubits or registers, then run entire circuits on simulators or real quantum hardware. This layered abstraction hides the linear algebraic complexity while preserving the programmatic intuition of classical programming.

No quantum program is complete without *measurement*, the process by which quantum superpositions collapse into classical information that can be read and further processed. Measuring a qubit forces it into one of the basis states, typically $|0\rangle$ or $|1\rangle$, with probabilities determined by the state's amplitudes prior to measurement. In code, measurement routines return classical outcomes, often as bits or boolean values, thereby bridging quantum data back into the classical world. Because measurement is inherently probabilistic and destructive, it must be applied judiciously within a circuit.

An essential nuance is the integration of *hybrid classical control* into quantum programs. Classical computers, which control quantum devices, monitor measurement results and make decisions such as which gates to apply next, adapting the circuit dynamically. This interplay of classical feedback with quantum operations is why modern quantum software often looks like a dance of intertwined classical and quantum instructions, leveraging strengths of both paradigms.

To crystallize these ideas, imagine constructing a simple circuit to generate an entangled pair of qubits—known as a Bell state—and then measure them. In pseudocode:

```
qreg = allocate_qubits(2)
apply(H, qreg[0])       // Create superposition on qubit 0
apply(CNOT, control=qreg[0], target=qreg[1])
// Entangle the pair
result0 = measure(qreg[0])
result1 = measure(qreg[1])
```

This snippet embodies the essence of quantum programming: initializing and grouping qubits, applying single and controlled gates to manipulate their joint state, and finally extracting classical outcomes. The measured results will be correlated—if `result0` is 0, `result1` is very likely 0, and similarly for 1—revealing the telltale signature of entanglement, accessible by just a few lines of code.

In sum, the quantum circuit model, when scaffolded by qubit abstractions, gate operations, multi-qubit registers, and measurement mechanics, provides a versatile and rich programming paradigm. Far from arcane mathematical formalism, it offers a hands-on, almost tangible way to harness quantum phenomena for computation. By understanding these core primitives and how they interconnect, one gains both the language and intuition to explore the frontiers of quantum algorithms, where computing transcends classic boundaries not through brute force but through the subtle art of quantum state choreography.

6.2 Introduction to Quantum Algorithms

Quantum algorithms lie at the heart of the revolutionary promise of quantum communication. They translate the abstract principles of quantum mechanics into concrete steps that enable secure information exchange, entanglement distribution, and quantum data processing. Understanding how these algorithms are structured, implemented, and optimized in software reveals not only their elegance but also the practical challenges involved in harnessing quantum phenomena for communication tasks.

At the core of any quantum algorithm is a familiar three-phase structure: initialization, unitary evolution, and measurement. The *initialization* phase prepares qubits in well-defined quantum states, often starting with pure states such as the computational basis states $|0\rangle$ or $|1\rangle$. This initialization sets the stage for processing quantum information. Next comes the *unitary evolution* phase, where the qubits undergo carefully designed quantum gates—reversible transformations that manipulate their probability amplitudes without losing coherence. Finally, the *measurement* phase collapses the quantum state into classical information, extracting the algorithm's output. Together, these phases form the skeleton upon which quantum communication routines are built, dictating how information is encoded, manipulated, and ultimately read out.

To appreciate the practical significance of this algorithmic structure, consider the BB84 quantum key distribution protocol, a flagship example of quantum communication. BB84 revolves around securely sharing a cryptographic key by encoding bits onto qubits in different bases. Software implementations of BB84 meticulously reproduce its essential steps: *state preparation*, where each bit is encoded into either the rectilinear $\{|0\rangle, |1\rangle\}$ or diagonal $\{|+\rangle, |-\rangle\}$ basis; *basis selection* by both sender and receiver, introducing intrinsic quantum uncertainty; and finally *measurement* in chosen bases. The crucial *sifting* step follows, where sender and receiver compare their bases classically to discard incompatible measurements, leaving a shared subset of bits whose privacy is guaranteed by quantum principles. Coding this protocol highlights how algorithm design intertwines physics and classical logic—quantum state manipulations and conditional classical processing coalesce into a secure communication channel.

Beyond key distribution, quantum communication employs more sophisticated routines such as *quantum teleportation*, a protocol that enables the transfer of an unknown quantum state from one location to another without physically sending the qubit itself. Implementing teleportation in software requires orchestrating a few key operations: first, establishing an entangled pair shared between sender and receiver, which acts as a quantum channel. Then, the sender performs a *Bell measurement* on the qubit to be teleported together with their half of the entangled pair, projecting the combined system onto a maximally entangled basis. This measurement yields classical bits that the sender transmits via a classical channel. Finally, the receiver applies *Pauli corrections* contingent on those bits to recover the original quantum state. Each step corresponds to distinct subroutines in code, with entanglement generation, joint measurement, and conditional gates forming reusable components. Teleportation therefore embodies the modular and interactive nature of quantum algorithms, blending quantum operations with classical communication and control.

Superdense coding complements teleportation by utilizing shared entanglement to send two classical bits through a single qubit. This counterintuitive feat hinges on encoding: the sender applies specific quantum gates to their half of an entangled pair, effectively imprinting two bits of information onto one qubit. The receiver then performs a joint measurement to decode the bits. In software frameworks, superdense coding routines involve implementing state preparation, entanglement, encoding gates, and measurement—all encapsulated within neat function calls that mirror the protocol's

163

conceptual steps. This procedure illustrates how quantum correlations boost communication capacity beyond classical limits.

No discussion of quantum communication is complete without addressing errors, an ever-present obstacle in fragile quantum states. Here, *error-correction* subroutines become indispensable. A simple example involves encoding a logical qubit into multiple physical qubits to protect against bit-flip or phase-flip errors. Software simulations recreate these codes by initializing multiple qubits, executing entangling gates to generate redundancy, and performing *syndrome measurements* that diagnose errors without collapsing the encoded information. These routines form the backbone of fault-tolerant quantum communication, allowing protocols to run reliably in imperfect conditions. Even rudimentary error correction reveals the interplay between conceptual theory and implementation complexity that pervades quantum algorithms.

Amplifying success probabilities often requires *amplitude amplification*, a valuable technique generalized from Grover's search algorithm. By applying carefully designed quantum reflections, this method increases the amplitude of desired states, boosting the likelihood of favorable measurement outcomes in probabilistic subroutines. Incorporating amplitude amplification into communication software involves inserting iterative unitary operations interleaved with phase flips, tailoring these sequences to the task at hand. This strategic amplification demonstrates how quantum algorithms— though probabilistic—can be engineered to optimize performance and reliability.

Given the multifaceted nature of quantum communication protocols, *modular algorithm design* emerges as a natural and effective programming paradigm.

By decomposing protocols into discrete, reusable components—such as state preparation modules, entanglement distribution routines, measurement engines, and classical post-processing functions—software gains clarity, flexibility, and maintainability. This modularity not only facilitates debugging and extension but also reflects the layered architecture of quantum communication stacks, where physical qubits, logical qubits, and classical interfaces coexist.

Evaluating and optimizing these algorithms demands rigorous tracking of *resource and performance metrics*. In simulations, key indicators include the number of qubits employed, gate depth (the number of sequential gate layers), fidelity (a measure of state accuracy), and runtime. Monitoring these metrics guides algorithm refinement, revealing bottlenecks in circuit complexity or coherence times and informing engineering choices for scalable quantum communications. The integration of abstract protocols with these quantitative measures ensures that quantum algorithms remain grounded in technological realities.

To facilitate analysis during execution, software implementations frequently embed *logging and telemetry hooks*. These callbacks record measurement outcomes, gate operations, timing, and error events in real-time, providing indispensable insight into the algorithm's internal dynamics. Beyond mere debugging, such telemetry supports statistical validation, performance benchmarking, and the development of adaptive quantum controls. In effect, they turn the execution of quantum communication routines into a transparent, data-rich process, enabling iterative improvements.

Translating quantum communication algorithms from theoretical constructs into software modules reveals a fascinating tapestry woven from physics, computer science, and engineering. The journey from abstract qubits and gates to coded subroutines brings into focus the subtle balances—between quantum and classical information, between probabilistic measurement and deterministic control, and between hardware constraints and logical design—that define this field. With tools like BB84 key distribution, teleportation, and superdense coding implemented as software routines, and supported by error correction, amplitude amplification, and modular architecture, the repertoire of quantum communication algorithms becomes both accessible and practicable. These foundations not only open doors for secure communication in a quantum future but also exemplify the profound synergy of theory and implementation that defines modern quantum information science.

6.3 Quantum Simulators and Software

The burgeoning field of quantum networks, promising secure communication and unprecedented computing power, confronts a fundamental challenge: real quantum hardware remains scarce, costly, and delicate. This scarcity elevates the role of quantum simulators—software platforms that emulate quantum devices and communication channels—allowing researchers and developers to design, test, and refine quantum network protocols long before deploying them on physical systems. By mimicking quantum behavior digitally, simulators provide a sandbox to explore the mysterious quantum realm with classical computers, enabling critical insights, debugging, and performance evaluation without the expense and fragility of hardware experiments.

Among the most prominent and accessible tools

for quantum development is *Qiskit*, an open-source software development kit released by IBM. Written in Python, Qiskit offers an elegant interface to construct quantum circuits using an intuitive circuit builder, facilitates optimization and adaptation of these circuits via a transpiler, and provides access to real quantum back-ends as well as highly accurate simulators. Notably, Qiskit allows developers to tailor their software closely to hardware constraints, bridging the gap between idealized algorithms and practical implementations. Its growing ecosystem includes modules for noise modeling, error correction, and even quantum chemistry, making it a versatile option for those eager to experiment with various quantum computing paradigms.

Complementing Qiskit, Google's *Cirq* framework targets the peculiarities of Noisy Intermediate-Scale Quantum (NISQ) devices—the current generation of imperfect quantum machines. Cirq's strength lies in its flexibility, enabling programmers to design complex quantum circuits that explicitly incorporate noise and hardware-specific constraints. Unlike some more abstract platforms, Cirq embraces the experimental nature of quantum hardware, providing detailed control of gate operations and sophisticated scheduling. This focus allows users to simulate realistic quantum processes, crucial for evaluating algorithms under the conditions they will actually face, and to benchmark performances rigorously.

While Qiskit and Cirq excel at simulating isolated quantum processors, quantum networks demand temporal precision and intricate link modeling. This is where specialized simulators like *NetSquid* distinguish themselves. Developed specifically for quantum network protocols, NetSquid simulates the precise timing of quantum operations and classical communication, enabling accurate representation of entanglement distribution, quantum memories, and multiplexed channels. It integrates detailed physical models—photon loss, decoherence, and hardware latency—making it an indispensable tool for analyzing complex networking scenarios. In this domain, NetSquid offers developers a 'time machine' to test and optimize the intricate dance of qubits across distances, capturing phenomena that simpler simulators often abstract away.

Setting up these frameworks demands a modest but deliberate configuration process. Python environments with compatible versions, package dependencies, and sometimes hardware-specific drivers form the usual foundation. Qiskit and Cirq installation typically involves standard Python package managers such as `pip`, while NetSquid may require additional compilation steps or dependencies to support its rigorous timing simulations. Once installed, these tools need connections to simulators or physical quantum processors—Qiskit links seamlessly to IBM's cloud back-ends, Cirq offers integration with Google's quantum processors, and NetSquid runs primarily on classical hardware emulating quantum networks. Each framework provides comprehensive documentation and tutorials to smooth this initial setup, encouraging experimentation by lowering technical barriers.

Despite their differing aims, these frameworks share common API design patterns that help unify the developer experience. Central to them is the concept of a *qubit object*—an abstraction representing the fundamental quantum bit, capable of holding superpositions and entanglement. Developers construct *circuits* or *protocols* by applying gates, measurements, and other operations to these qubits in a stepwise manner. Simulators then execute these circuits, generating outputs ranging from measurement outcomes to fidelity estimates. This familiar paradigm allows programmers to write hardware-agnostic code that can be translated, optimized, and tested across multiple back-ends, facilitating comparative studies and iterative improvements.

A direct comparison highlights how these frameworks carve out distinct niches and capabilities within the quantum software landscape:

Feature	Qiskit	Cirq	NetSquid
Primary Focus	Quantum computing, gate-level circuits	NISQ device programming	Quantum network protocol simulation
Noise	Device-specific noise models, configurable	Flexible noise modeling, hardware-aware	Detailed channel and memory noise, timing effects
Network Support	Limited (mostly single-processor)	Basic multi-device support	Comprehensive network topology, timing accuracy
Back-ends	IBM quantum processors, simulators	Google quantum processors, simulators	Simulator only
Programming Language	Python	Python	Python, with C++ core
Typical Use Cases	Algorithm development, error correction	Experimental gate optimization, benchmarking	Quantum key distribution, entanglement routing

Consider an example workflow typical of quantum network research: simulating a quantum key distribution (QKD) protocol. The developer begins by defining qubit objects representing photons transmitted between nodes. Using a circuit constructor, they encode the protocol's operations—preparing states, applying gates, performing measurements—and insert noise models to mimic real-world imperfections. A logging mechanism records intermediate states and detection events. Running the simulation involves stepping through these instructions in the simulator, with the software tracking timing and probabilistic outcomes. By analyzing the results—such as error rates and key generation speed—the researcher can iterate on code and parameters to enhance protocol performance before eventual deployment on hardware or real networks.

As quantum simulators become more sophisticated, embracing best practices enhances their utility and reliability. Choosing the right simulator depends on the task complexity: Qiskit or Cirq can suffice for algorithmic and gate-level explorations, while NetSquid better serves timing-critical network protocols. Incorporating noise models calibrated to physical devices ensures simulations remain faithful to reality, avoiding overly optimistic predictions. Scaling tests progressively from small circuits or short network paths to larger systems reveals bottlenecks and computational overhead early. Rigorous logging and visualization help interpret probabilistic quantum behavior, fostering transparency and reproducibility. Collaboration between tool developers and quantum engineers further refines simulation accuracy and usability.

The expanding universe of quantum simulators and software is not merely a convenience but a necessity, enabling innovation while circumventing the fragility and expense of hardware experiments. By selecting appropriate frameworks, mastering their APIs, and applying thoughtful noise and timing models, developers bridge theory and practice, navigating the quantum frontier with confidence. Equipped with these digital laboratories, we prepare for the moment when simulated qubits seamlessly transition to physical ones, ushering in the quantum internet era.

6.4 Building Blocks of Quantum Protocols in Code

Quantum communication protocols are more than theoretical constructs; they are lived processes executed step-by-step by software carefully crafted to manipulate delicate quantum states while coordinating information flow across classical channels. To translate abstract concepts into functioning quantum networks, engineers and scientists rely on a suite of core software patterns— reusable, modular code structures that embody the essential operations of quantum communication. These building blocks form a robust foundation upon which complex protocols are assembled, tested, and scaled. Exploring them illuminates how quantum ideas become tangible and reveals the practical artistry behind orchestrating trembling qubits in a noisy world.

The journey begins with *Qubit Pool Management*, a crucial pattern that addresses the ephemeral nature of qubits. Unlike classical bits, qubits cannot be copied freely, and their coherence fades over time. Therefore, a quantum program must dynamically allocate and release qubits based on need, managing a finite "pool" of available qubits across the duration of an entire protocol. Imagine a quantum memory bank where qubits are checked out, used for encoding or measurement, then returned or discarded to free up precious resources. This dynamic allocation avoids both waste and deadlock, ensuring the system adapts fluidly as operations progress. Without careful pool management, a protocol risks stalling because no qubits are free or, conversely, squandering them on redundant tasks.

At the heart of many quantum communication schemes is the *Entangled-Pair Factory*, a specialized routine responsible for generating pairs of entangled qubits—usually Bell pairs—and distributing each half to different network endpoints. Entanglement is the quintessential quantum resource powering phenomena such as teleportation and superdense coding; however, creating and sharing these entangled pairs secretly is nontrivial. The factory encapsulates this complexity, often interfacing with physical hardware or simulators to produce high-fidelity Bell pairs on demand. Its design balances efficiency, error handling, and synchronization, because a failed pair must be discarded and recreated without disrupting the protocol's broader flow.

Once entanglement and qubit management are handled, protocols like BB84—the pioneering quantum key distribution scheme—are implemented through dedicated software modules. A *BB84 Module* encapsulates the preparation, transmission, and sifting stages of this protocol into a coherent class or object. It manages the random selection of basis states to encode bits, controls the timing and sending of qubits, and processes classical communication to reconcile measurement bases and extract the secret key. By bundling these steps, the module becomes a reusable, composable element that can be tested independently or integrated into larger systems. This layering of logic mirrors how BB84's conceptual stages have inspired a generation of quantum cryptography software.

Quantum teleportation, often the poster child of quantum communication magic, also inspires a canonical coding pattern: the *Teleportation Function*. This encapsulates the sequence of operations—performing a Bell-state measurement on the sender's side, transmitting the classical measurement results,

172

and applying conditional correction operations at the receiver's side. Encapsulating teleportation as a reusable routine abstracts away the intricate interplay of quantum measurement and classical messaging, enabling higher-level protocols to invoke it as a primitive building block. This modularity proves invaluable as teleportation finds new applications in error correction, distributed quantum computing, and network repeater designs.

Extending the entanglement horizon beyond point-to-point links requires the *Entanglement Swapping Method*. Here, intermediate nodes perform Bell measurements on pairs of entangled qubits they hold, effectively connecting remote endpoints by "swapping" entanglement. This operation is more than a quantum trick—it forms the backbone of quantum repeaters that enable long-distance quantum communication. Implementing this pattern involves intricate choreography: the method must trigger Bell measurements, await heralding signals confirming successful operations, and update the network state accordingly. Callbacks or event handlers often tie into the method to synchronize classical and quantum states, ensuring the entanglement chain remains intact despite probabilistic failures.

Quantum communication is inherently a hybrid dance of quantum particles and classical messages. The *Classical Communication Interface* layer abstracts the protocols' classical messaging needs—sending instructions, measurement results, and acknowledgments alongside qubit transmissions. This interface offers APIs that shield higher-level code from network or transport details, managing queues, timeouts, and retransmissions. It makes it possible to blend quantum and classical operations seamlessly, preserving the tight coordination required for reliable protocol execution.

173

Keeping this hybrid choreography in sync across geographically separated nodes calls for *Event-Driven Coordination*. Software leverages message handlers, asynchronous callbacks, or event loops to respond to incoming classical messages, quantum measurement outcomes, or environmental signals. This reactive programming model allows nodes to progress independently yet remain electronically "in tune," handling asynchrony, delays, and failures gracefully. Event-driven architectures turn the inherently probabilistic timing of quantum operations into manageable, orderly progressions.

To build maintainable and scalable quantum software, *Modular Library Design* is indispensable. Quantum communication protocols, utilities, and interfaces are bundled into well-defined packages or libraries, each with clear responsibilities and interfaces. This modularity supports code reuse across projects, collaboration between research teams, and rapid prototyping of new features. Just as classical software matured through reusable libraries and frameworks, quantum software is now following suit—enabling the community to build on shared foundations rather than reinventing the wheel.

The final piece in preparing robust quantum software is *Testing Stubs and Mocks*, essential tools borrowed from classical software engineering. Given the technical and financial challenges of real quantum hardware, developers simulate remote nodes, channels, and noisy environments using mocked objects or stubs. These test doubles mimic the behavior of physical systems, allowing local unit tests of protocols and communication patterns without waiting for fragile experimental setups. Such rigor accelerates development, improves code quality, and builds confidence before deployment on actual quantum networks.

Together, these software patterns integrate the abstract principles of quantum communication into functioning, extensible, and testable codebases. They transform quantum ideas—from entanglement generation to key distribution—into practical instructions that machines can execute reliably. Understanding these building blocks provides an indispensable glimpse into the craftsmanship powering tomorrow's quantum internet.

6.5 Error Handling and Debugging

Hybrid quantum computing—where classical and quantum elements intertwine—introduces a fascinating but formidable challenge: how to identify and resolve faults in code that bridges two fundamentally different realms. Unlike classical software development, where errors are typically logical or syntactic missteps, hybrid quantum code faces a double-edged sword of bugs. These arise not only from programming slips but also from the intrinsic noise and imperfections characteristic of today's quantum hardware. Untangling these intertwined error sources is the first crucial step toward reliable quantum software.

- **Error Sources**

  In hybrid quantum programming, errors fall broadly into two camps. The first comprises logical bugs—mistakes in the sequence or logic of quantum gate applications, measurement protocols, or classical control flow. These errors echo the familiar problems in traditional software: typos, misordered commands, or incorrect parameter values. The second camp, however, is more elusive and stems from the intimate

175

physical reality of quantum devices: noise and decoherence. Quantum bits (qubits) are notoriously fragile, with errors creeping in as environmental disturbances, imperfect gate operations, or spontaneous qubit relaxation. Unlike classical bits, which are digital and stable, quantum information degrades continuously, producing stochastic errors that simulators must carefully model and programmers must strive to mitigate.

Distinguishing logical bugs from hardware-induced noise requires meticulous testing strategies and a nuanced understanding of the system's behavior. Without this clarity, debugging efforts may chase phantom errors or misattribute hardware faults to software mistakes—frustrations that have long haunted early quantum programmers.

- **Noise Injection Models**

  To grapple with hardware imperfections, developers rely on noise injection models incorporated into quantum simulators. These models simulate relevant error mechanisms—such as bit-flip and phase-flip errors, amplitude damping, or depolarizing noise—offering a virtual laboratory to observe how circuits degrade under realistic conditions. By configuring these models with parameters like coherence times or gate fidelities, one can recreate the fuzzy quantum landscape inside a classical environment.

  This approach allows for early detection of protocols that are overly sensitive to noise and supports error mitigation strategies before committing to costly experiments on actual devices. Noise injection transforms simulators from perfect mathematical abstractions into plausible stand-ins for the messy quantum world, providing critical insight for debugging and optimization.

- **Unit Testing Circuits**

Borrowing a page from classical software engineering, unit testing in quantum circuits involves specifying test cases that target individual components—be it a single gate sequence, an entanglement operation, or a measurement protocol branch. These tests verify that each fragment performs its expected function, ideally in isolation, thereby limiting the complexity of the debugging task.

For example, if a teleportation protocol is misbehaving, writing a test that checks fidelity after the entangling step or the classical feedforward can isolate the faulty segment. Unit tests serve as checkpoints where calculations are verified before they cascade into larger faults, instilling confidence that the quantum code is correct at the building-block level.

- **Circuit Visualization**

With the abstract and often counterintuitive nature of quantum operations, visual aids become invaluable debugging tools. Circuit diagrams render sequences of gates into familiar, ordered pictures, while state-vector visualizations chart the evolution of quantum states through complex amplitudes and probabilities.

These representations help programmers trace the expected versus actual transformations

177

of qubits step-by-step, making discrepancies more tangible. Visual inspection often reveals misaligned gates, improper qubit mappings, or unintended entanglement, which might be invisible when only looking at raw code or textual data. In practice, visualization bridges human intuition with quantum abstraction, a critical fusion for effective debugging.

- **Logging and Tracing**

  While visualizations provide snapshots, logging and tracing capture a detailed chronicle of execution. By instrumenting hybrid quantum code with log statements that record gate operations, measurement outcomes, and classical control decisions, developers create a timeline that chronicles the program's behavior during runtime.

  This detailed data allows post-execution analysis to identify when and where things diverge from expectations, particularly in complex multi-qubit or feedback-driven protocols. Combining logs with simulator outputs or hardware results helps pinpoint rare or context-dependent faults that might evade simpler tests. Effective logging transforms the execution of a quantum program from a mysterious black box to a transparent process amenable to inspection.

- **Assertion Checks**

  Inserting assertions into hybrid quantum programs—statements that check specific conditions or thresholds during execution—is a proactive strategy to catch anomalies as soon as they arise. Assertions may verify that the fidelity of a quantum state remains above a critical level, that measurement probabilities conform to physical constraints, or that classical variables fall within expected ranges after quantum operations.

When an assertion fails, it serves as an early-warning beacon signaling that either the implementation is flawed or the error environment has overwhelmed the protocol. These embedded sanity checks prevent silent propagation of errors and aid developers in localizing faults within probabilistic processes that otherwise yield noisy outputs.

- **Parameter Sweeps**

  Debugging quantum code is rarely a one-shot affair. Often, it requires systematically exploring how variations in parameters influence outcomes. Parameter sweeps automate this process by varying error rates, gate durations, or protocol-specific settings across a range of values and observing the resulting performance.

  For instance, sweeping depolarizing noise rates in a simulator can reveal thresholds beyond which a quantum error correcting code fails, or varying timing delays in control pulses can uncover timing-sensitive bugs. Through these controlled experiments, developers gain a landscape perspective, identifying robust operating regions and vulnerability points. Parameter sweeps transform debugging from reactive patching to exploratory tuning.

- **Exception Handling Patterns**

  Hybrid quantum systems stack complex layers of dependencies—from classical software

179

environments to quantum hardware access—so unexpected failures can arise from resource exhaustion, connectivity loss, or internal simulator errors. Designing robust exception handling patterns means anticipating these eventualities and implementing graceful recovery mechanisms.

Rather than allowing abrupt crashes that waste computational resources or obscure root causes, well-crafted exception handlers capture error context, provide informative diagnostics, and attempt fallback strategies wherever possible. This resilience is especially important in long-running experiments or cloud-based quantum services where intermittent failures are commonplace. Exception handling shapes a smooth debugging journey through a bumpy computational terrain.

- **Reproducibility Practices**

  Quantum computations often incorporate randomness—whether through initial state preparation, measurement, or noise simulation—so ensuring reproducible results is paramount for debugging and scientific rigor. Managing random seeds explicitly, documenting software and hardware versions, and specifying environment configurations ensures that runs can be faithfully reproduced.

  Version control systems track code changes and prevent inadvertent regressions, while containerization and environment specification mitigate subtle differences in dependencies that might alter execution. These best practices transform the chaotic process of debugging into a disciplined investigation, enabling comparative analysis across different code versions and hardware backends.

- **Synthesis of Best Practices**

  Navigating error handling and debugging in hybrid quantum code demands an integrated workflow. Begin by isolating logical errors through unit testing and assertion checks, complemented by visualization to connect abstract operations with concrete intuition. Introduce noise injection models to anticipate hardware-induced faults early, using parameter sweeps to chart performance under varying conditions. Employ comprehensive logging and tracing to gather detailed empirical data, and implement robust exception handling to maintain resilience in the face of unexpected failures. Finally, uphold rigorous reproducibility practices to cement confidence that debugging insights are genuine and repeatable.

  Together, these techniques form a rich toolkit that tackles quantum programming's unique challenges head-on. While the quantum frontier remains experimentally demanding and conceptually complex, methodical debugging transforms it from a realm of mystifying failures into a landscape suited for exploration, innovation, and eventual mastery.

6.6 Open-Source Quantum Networking Projects

The evolution of quantum networking from theoretical concept to experimental reality owes much to a vibrant ecosystem of open-source projects. These community-driven platforms and libraries empower researchers, developers, and enthusiasts alike to simulate, build, and refine quantum communication protocols with unprecedented accessibility. Bringing together collaborative spirit and cutting-edge technology, they form the digital backbone upon which future quantum internet technologies are being prototyped and tested.

Among the pioneering tools fostering this openness is *NetSquid*, a quantum network simulator hosted on GitHub that has steadily become a cornerstone for researchers worldwide. Designed with modularity and extensibility in mind, NetSquid models the architecture of realistic quantum networks—encompassing qubits, quantum memories, entanglement operations, and classical communication channels—all within a discrete-event simulation framework. Its core strength lies in its hybrid approach: allowing detailed simulation of quantum states alongside the classical network protocols that govern them. This dual perspective is crucial because quantum networks do not merely transmit qubits but must intricately coordinate measurement outcomes, error correction, and routing decisions. For newcomers eager to contribute or explore, NetSquid's GitHub repository offers comprehensive documentation, example scripts, and an active issue tracker where community engagement flourishes.

Parallel to NetSquid is *SimulaQron*, a framework uniquely focused on emulating quantum networks over virtual infrastructures. Where traditional simulators operate in a monolithic environment, SimulaQron creates a distributed landscape of interconnected nodes, each simulating local quantum processors communicating via classical channels. This virtual-ization enables developers to test quantum network applications in conditions more representative of real-world deployments. By bridging simulated quantum hardware and classical networking stacks, SimulaQron facilitates the development of distributed quantum software protocols such as teleportation, entanglement swapping, and error correction distributed across nodes. The framework's design encourages incremental development: users can start with basic quantum applications and progressively scale towards complex, multi-node scenarios, effectively simulating the transition from science fiction to real quantum internet systems.

Complementing these simulation environments is *QuNetSim*, a Python-based toolkit crafted to simplify the creation and execution of quantum network protocols. QuNetSim offers intuitive abstractions allowing users to define network nodes, quantum channels, and classical communication paths without delving into hardware specifics. Its appeal lies in striking a balance between ease of use and functional depth: educational users can experiment with fundamental protocols like BB84 quantum key distribution (QKD) or superdense coding, while advanced researchers can extend the platform to prototype novel algorithms or layering strategies. This adaptability is supported by active community contributions hosted on public repositories, where shared examples, bug reports, and feature requests accelerate the toolkit's maturation.

Real-world quantum key distribution requires more than just protocol design—it demands rigorous benchmarking to gauge performance under practical conditions. Addressing this need, the *OpenQK Suite* exists as a specialized open-source collection offering benchmarking tools tailored for QKD implementations. OpenQK enables users to evaluate key generation rates, error thresholds, and robustness against eavesdropping under varied network configurations. By providing detailed key-rate analysis and statistical visualization, the suite serves both experimentalists tuning laboratory setups and theorists validating security claims. OpenQK's openness encourages transparency and reproducibility, essential qualities as industries and governments increasingly consider QKD for secure communications.

While individual projects excel at simulation, emulation, and benchmarking, the broader community recognizes that a future quantum internet must adhere to standardized protocols to ensure interoperability and scalability. This imperative motivated the development of the *Quantum Internet Stack* (*QIS*), an ambitious collaborative effort to define modular protocol layers much like the classical TCP/IP model. The QIS initiative breaks down the quantum internet architecture into manageable strata—including physical qubit transmission, entanglement generation, error correction, routing, and application interfaces—which can evolve independently yet function cohesively. Regularly updated on open platforms, QIS invites multidisciplinary contributions spanning physics, computer science, and engineering, providing a framework where innovation and standardization reinforce one another.

Open-source quantum networking projects thrive not only on groundbreaking code but also on well-crafted guidelines that nurture communal growth. Clear *contribution guidelines* standardize the process for reporting issues, submitting pull requests, and proposing enhancements, fostering a welcoming environment for developers of all skill levels. These guidelines emphasize best practices such as writing descriptive commit messages, adhering to established coding styles, and engaging respectfully with peers during code reviews. The collective adherence to such protocols elevates project quality and accelerates progress, turning many isolated efforts into cohesive collaborations.

Accessibility extends beyond code to *documentation and examples*, indispensable resources that demystify complex concepts and accelerate onboarding. Most projects dedicate extensive repositories to tutorials that walk users through fundamental and advanced functionalities, accompanied by comprehensive API references. Interactive Jupyter notebooks often showcase live code demonstrations, providing a hands-on experience that bridges theoretical descriptions with practical experimentation. The availability of such educational assets empowers newcomers to transcend passive observation and become active participants in quantum networking development.

The social dimensions of open-source ecosystems are equally vital. *Community channels* such as dedicated forums, mailing lists, and real-time chat groups on platforms like Discord or Slack act as living incubators for ideas and troubleshooting. Here, novices can seek guidance, experts can debate emerging techniques, and collaborations can spark organically across continents. These dynamic discussions not only solve immediate technical problems but also chart the strategic direction of projects and crystallize shared visions for the quantum internet's future.

To solidify bonds and accelerate momentum, vibrant *events and workshops* are routinely organized. Hackathons invite developers to tackle predefined challenges, often resulting in innovative proof-of-concept implementations that might otherwise languish on wish lists. Tutorials at conferences and online webinars disseminate knowledge across disciplinary boundaries, equipping participants with up-to-date skills. Collaborative coding sprints offer concentrated bursts of development, where focused teams refine features and polish documentation. These in-person and virtual gatherings transform individual enthusiasm into collective achievement, reinforcing the open-source quantum networking community's resilience and creativity.

Together, these projects and community structures form a fertile arena for anyone curious about the quantum internet. By providing accessible tools, transparent protocols, and inclusive forums, they lower the barriers to entry and accelerate the collective journey toward a functioning quantum network. Prospective contributors need only pick a project that resonates, dive into the wealth of tutorials and documentation, and engage with the friendly, driven communities that underlie these initiatives. In doing so, they become active architects of a revolutionary technology destined to reshape how information moves across the world.

Chapter 7

Real World Applications of Quantum Internet

This chapter explores how quantum networking technologies are beginning to impact key sectors by offering unparalleled security, performance, and collaborative capabilities. We examine concrete use cases in finance, healthcare, government and defense, industry and smart infrastructure, and education and research. Each section highlights domain-specific challenges, quantum-enabled solutions, prototype deployments, and critical considerations for integrating quantum Internet services into real-world environments.

7.1 Financial Security and Banking

Modern finance operates on a knife-edge where vast transactions are executed in milliseconds, and the sanctity of each data packet determines fortunes and trust. Yet beneath this invisible dance of numbers lies a growing tension: the relentless escalation of cyber threats targeting banking infrastructures. Contemporary financial networks face a barrage of attack vectors, ranging from sophisticated phishing campaigns and malware intrusions to supply chain vulnerabilities and insider threats, all aimed at compromising transaction integrity, siphoning confidential data, or disrupting services. The stakes are immense; beyond financial loss, breaches erode public confidence and destabilize entire economies. Traditional cryptographic methods, while robust today, risk obsolescence as quantum computing looms on the horizon, threatening to unravel conventional encryption and expose financial secrets.

In this precarious landscape, quantum technologies offer a compelling evolution, particularly through Quantum Key Distribution (QKD), which harnesses the laws of quantum physics to guarantee secrecy. Unlike classical encryption reliant on computational complexity, QKD generates cryptographic keys using quantum states of photons, ensuring that any eavesdropping attempt irreversibly alters these states and becomes immediately detectable. When applied to high-value fund transfers and interbank communications, QKD transforms security from an assumption into a provable fact. Imagine two banks exchanging encryption keys over a quantum channel instead of the internet: this procedure not only prevents interception but also reassures both parties that their transaction remains untampered, thereby reinforcing trust at the foundation of financial exchanges.

Speed is another axis where quantum links can redefine finance, especially in algorithmic trading ecosystems where fractions of a second determine profitability. Conventional security protocols introduce latency due to encryption overheads and verification delays, creating a tension between speed and safety. Quantum links enable secure, low-latency connections that dramatically shrink this tradeoff. By detecting minute tampering gestures in quantum states, they provide instant alerts to any malicious interference, preventing corrupted data from skewing trading algorithms. This rapid tampering detection fortifies trading networks against both external intrusions and subtle internal manipulations, ensuring that decisions rest on authentic, unaltered information.

Beyond trading floors, the typical financial labyrinth of clearinghouses and settlement desks contends with cumbersome delays caused by multi-party reconciliations and fraud checks. Quantum communication channels open the possibility of near-instantaneous settlement mechanisms with end-to-end confidentiality. By continually refreshing cryptographic keys via QKD during the entire settlement window, financial institutions can maintain a secure handshake that protects transaction details from prying eyes. This continuous quantum linkage effectively seals the clearing process within an impregnable cryptographic envelope, reducing settlement times from days to moments and shrinking counterparty risk. Such a breakthrough not only enhances liquidity but also mitigates systemic risks by ensuring each payment finality is both instantaneous and indisputable.

The challenges multiply when money crosses borders, traversing complex networks layered with differing regulations, infrastructures, and potential points of compromise. Cross-border payment protocols often rely on multiple intermediaries, each a potential vulnerability. Quantum-secured international payment lines can shield these transactions against eavesdropping and fraud, preserving privacy between originating and receiving banks regardless of routing complexities. By embedding quantum keys within existing communication frameworks, payments become resilient to interception and replay attacks, even in environments hostile to conventional cybersecurity.

This approach could usher in a new era of global
financial interoperability, where speed and privacy
coalesce despite geopolitical or infrastructural
disparities.

As quantum-secure financial solutions emerge,
regulatory bodies and standard-setting organizations
grapple with adapting legal frameworks and compliance
requirements. The transition from classical to quantum-
resistant cryptography challenges norms around data
protection, auditability, and operational transparency.
Industry groups are now collaborating to draft evolving
standards that codify quantum-resilient practices,
defining protocols, certification processes, and incident
responses tailored to quantum communications. These
efforts aim to balance technological innovation with
trust and accountability, ensuring that quantum
security meshes seamlessly with the stringent demands
of financial governance. The adoption of such
standards will be pivotal to widespread acceptance
and implementation, as institutions seek assurance
that quantum protections meet or exceed established
regulatory benchmarks.

Quantum links also synergize elegantly with blockchain
technologies, which underpin many emerging financial
applications including decentralized finance and smart
contracts. Distributed ledgers rely intrinsically on
immutability and transparency, but their cryptographic
security faces future threats from quantum adversaries.
Incorporating QKD-secured channels for transmitting
consensus messages or distributing ledger updates
creates a fortified layer that preserves tamper-proof
records while enhancing privacy. Hybrid quantum-
classical frameworks can safeguard not only the
ledger content but also the communication channels
connecting nodes, thwarting attempts to manipulate

transaction histories or disrupt consensus processes. This integration brings the best of both worlds— quantum-protected confidentiality with blockchain's decentralized trust.

Practical implementations of quantum-enhanced finance are already underway, as leading banks and financial consortia pilot fiber-based QKD systems linking data centers, trading floors, and central offices. These prototypes reveal not only the viability but also the nuanced complexities of deploying quantum networks in live environments. For example, a major European bank demonstrated secure QKD-encrypted communication between two trading hubs, achieving stable key rates sufficient for continuous encryption of sensitive transactions. Such trials reveal critical lessons on network integration, environmental noise mitigation, and synchronization, paving the way for scalable quantum finance infrastructures. Each successful prototype brings closer the day when quantum-secured finance transitions from visionary concept to day-to-day reality.

Yet the path to widespread quantum security in banking is far from straightforward. Operational challenges abound, from managing the lifecycle of quantum keys to ensuring compatibility across diverse legacy systems and rapidly evolving quantum hardware. The cost implications are substantial, as quantum infrastructure demands specialized equipment like photon sources, detectors, and low-loss channels. Moreover, training personnel to understand and maintain quantum systems without compromising classical security protocols complicates adoption. Interoperability between quantum networks and classical cryptographic frameworks remains an ongoing engineering hurdle, as does the need for robust error correction to maintain key integrity over long distances. These realities reinforce that while quantum finance holds transformative promise, its journey is as much strategic and organizational as technological.

Bringing quantum links into finance signifies more than a technological upgrade; it represents a paradigm shift in how trust and security are conceived in an age of digital threats. By embedding fundamental physical principles into the fabric of financial communications, quantum technologies offer a future where transaction integrity, privacy, and system resilience are not assumptions but mathematically grounded guarantees. This infusion of quantum security transforms vulnerabilities into strengths and opens possibilities for innovation—be it instant settlements, fortified trading, or tamper-proof ledgers. As the financial world advances toward this quantum horizon, it rewrites the rules of security and fortifies the institutions that underpin global prosperity.

7.2 Healthcare Data and Research Collaboration

As healthcare becomes increasingly digitized, the sheer volume of sensitive medical information traversing global networks has soared to unprecedented levels. Patient records, genomic sequences, clinical trial results, and real-time diagnostics generate troves of data ripe for accelerating research but equally vulnerable to interception or tampering. In this landscape, the advent of quantum communication offers a transformative promise: harnessing the fundamental laws of physics to secure these exchanges, propelling collaboration without compromising privacy.

Patient Data Privacy At the core of healthcare lies the sanctity of patient confidentiality. Electronic health records (EHRs) are gold mines of personal and medical information, making their secure transfer and storage paramount. Traditional encryption methods, while robust today, face looming threats from quantum computing's potential to crack classical cryptographic codes. Quantum key distribution (QKD) preempts this challenge by enabling two parties to share encryption keys derived from quantum states of light, ensuring that any eavesdropping attempt disturbs these states and becomes instantly detectable. This ability to secure EHRs during transmission and maintain resilience against future computational advances elevates patient data privacy from a reactive defense to proactively impregnable protection.

Secure Multi-Site Clinical Trials Clinical trials often span multiple hospitals and research centers, requiring frequent synchronization and sharing of sensitive datasets. Ensuring that trial data remains unaltered and shielded from unauthorized eyes is critical both ethically and legally. Quantum channels facilitate the secure exchange of trial results and participant information with guaranteed confidentiality and integrity, overcoming vulnerabilities posed by classical networks. By connecting disparate institutions through a web of quantum links, researchers can coordinate complex randomized controlled trials or adaptive designs seamlessly, confident that the data's fidelity is maintained and tampering attempts thwarted at the quantum level.

Genomic Data Sharing Genomics epitomizes big data in medicine, where each human genome sequence—comprising billions of nucleotides—must be stored, processed, and often shared between institutions for comprehensive analyses. The challenge arises in preserving the confidentiality of this exquisitely personal information while leveraging its insights across research groups. Quantum-secured data links ensure that such high-volume genome sequencing collaborations do not expose individuals to risks of re-identification or unauthorized use. By applying QKD-based encryption to genomic data transfers, research consortia gain the dual advantage of speed and ironclad security, making personalized medicine's data-driven promises a practical reality.

Federated Learning Frameworks Machine learning has become an invaluable tool for extracting knowledge from complex medical data, but conventional training approaches demand centralized data access, raising privacy concerns. Federated learning circumvents this by enabling AI models to be trained collaboratively across multiple institutions without ever pooling raw data. When combined with QKD, federated learning frameworks achieve an unprecedented level of security: quantum keys encrypt the model updates transmitted between sites, mitigating risks of interception or manipulation. This marriage of quantum cryptography and distributed artificial intelligence transforms healthcare analytics, facilitating breakthroughs while respecting patient confidentiality and regulatory constraints.

Pharmaceutical Research Networks Pharmaceutical companies rely heavily on collaboration, sharing experimental findings and compound libraries with partners and contract research organizations. Intellectual property is the lifeblood of the industry, and leaks can lead to enormous financial and reputational damages. Quantum links offer a robust safeguard for these collaborations, encrypting interactions to prevent industrial espionage or data breaches. More than just a protective barrier, quantum-secured networks can accelerate joint development by fostering trust and enabling dynamic, real-time sharing of sensitive data streams, effectively creating a new paradigm for pharmaceutical innovation.

Remote Diagnostics and Telemedicine Healthcare delivery is evolving beyond hospital walls, with telemedicine and remote monitoring tools enabling patients to connect with providers anytime, anywhere. These streams of real-time physiological data are medically invaluable but also starkly vulnerable to interception. Quantum communication technologies safeguard these channels end-to-end, protecting continuous patient monitoring systems from data leaks or alterations. Such security assurances are crucial for maintaining patient trust and ensuring clinical decisions are based on untampered, authentic signals— particularly in critical care scenarios or for chronic disease management where rapid response depends on data integrity.

Data Integrity and Audit Trails Accurate documentation and traceability in healthcare are not optional; they underpin clinical decision-making, legal accountability, and regulatory compliance. Beyond confidentiality, the integrity of medical records and audit trails must be inviolable. Utilizing quantum-backed authentication methods, healthcare systems can implement immutable logging mechanisms whereby medical events—such as treatments, prescriptions, or diagnostic reports—are cryptographically timestamped and verifiable. This quantum leap in data provenance ensures that records cannot be altered retroactively, fostering transparency and trust in the entire healthcare ecosystem.

Infrastructure & Interoperability Integrating quantum

communication into existing hospital and research
infrastructures presents both technical and operational
challenges. Quantum nodes require careful deployment
within networks that must remain compatible with
legacy systems, ensuring seamless interoperability
across various platforms and protocols. Early
implementations demonstrate hybrid architectures
where quantum keys secure classical data traffic in a
layered approach, gradually augmenting traditional
networks without disruption. This pragmatic synthesis
allows healthcare organizations to harness quantum
security benefits immediately, while preparing for the
more comprehensive quantum internet anticipated in
the future.

Pilot Programs Several pioneering research consortia
exemplify the practical promise of quantum-secured
healthcare collaboration. Notably, pilot programs
spanning Europe and Asia have connected university
hospitals and research institutes via QKD-enabled
fibers, sharing anonymized clinical data and genomic
information to support large-scale studies on cancer
and rare diseases. These projects have successfully
demonstrated not only enhanced data security but also
operational feasibility, providing valuable lessons in
scaling, cost management, and multi-party governance.
Such early adopters are charting the course toward
widespread adoption and continuous innovation in
quantum-protected healthcare ecosystems.

Quantum communication is no longer a theoretical
luxury for the future; it is rapidly becoming an
indispensable tool for safeguarding the integrity,
privacy, and trustworthiness of healthcare data in
an interconnected world. By embedding quantum
links within the complex tapestry of medical research
and patient care, the healthcare community can

unlock unprecedented avenues for collaboration while protecting its most sensitive asset—the human body's intimate data. Building on centuries of medical advances, quantum technologies herald a new chapter where speed, security, and synergy coalesce to improve outcomes and redefine what it means to safeguard health in the digital age.

7.3 Secure Government and Military Communications

The strategic imperative of secrecy in government and military communications has never been more pressing. As adversaries develop increasingly sophisticated cyber tools and quantum computing inches closer to practical reality, the need to deploy quantum-hardened communication channels becomes paramount for preserving diplomatic integrity, operational security, and national defense. Quantum Key Distribution (QKD), underpinned by the fundamental laws of quantum mechanics, offers a radical shift in securing information flows, transforming how states communicate sensitive information across diplomatic posts, battlefields, and command centers.

Diplomatic Secure Links

Diplomatic missions, such as embassies and consulates, operate as nerve centers for international relations. Protecting them against covert interception or tampering is vital. Leveraging QKD-backed fiber optic links and satellite quantum channels, these facilities now benefit from encryption keys generated through quantum processes immune to eavesdropping. Unlike conventional cryptography, which depends on mathematical complexity, QKD security is guaranteed by quantum physics itself:

any attempt to intercept the quantum signal inevitably disturbs it, alerting parties to a breach.

In practical terms, metropolitan fiber optic networks connect embassies within capital cities, embedding quantum key generation directly into existing infrastructure. For instance, fiber-based QKD links in European capitals have begun securing diplomatic data flows, ensuring that critical communiqués or classified conversations remain confidential. Where fiber deployment is impractical—such as to remote consulates or during diplomatic missions in volatile regions—satellite QKD solutions offer a lifeline, enabling quantum-secure communications via free-space optical channels. Such hybrid quantum networks elevate diplomatic messaging to a new standard of security, mitigating risks of espionage and manipulation on the global stage.

Battlefield Networking

In contested environments, where communication lines may be jammed, tapped, or otherwise compromised, the resilience of military networking is paramount. Quantum-secured links offer more than theoretical protection; they provide robustness against advanced cyberattacks that threaten command, control, and situational awareness systems. Deploying mobile, ad-hoc quantum channels enables real-time exchange of keys between forward units and central command centers, ensuring tactical directives remain uncompromised.

Quantum links tailored for rugged terrains and battlefield conditions utilize compact QKD devices embedded within vehicular or airborne platforms. These devices can rapidly establish quantum keys over fiber, line-of-sight free-space optics, or even satellite relays, enhancing communication integrity under physical and electronic warfare pressures. By integrating quantum technologies with existing radio and optical systems, militaries achieve an unprecedented level of trust in the data that guides split-second decisions—where misinformation or interception could mean loss of life or mission failure.

Satellite QKD for Strategic Coverage

Extending quantum-secure communications beyond terrestrial infrastructure requires satellite-based QKD systems. These systems bridge vast geographic distances, connecting remote command posts, naval vessels, and mobile units in the field. Satellites equipped with quantum transmitters distribute keys via free-space channels with minimal latency and high security assurances.

Such systems overcome the limitations of fiber optics, which suffer losses over long distances and are vulnerable to physical damages or restrictions. Satellite QKD networks enable a strategic overlay, maintaining continuous, secure links across diverse theaters of operation—from arctic outposts to oceanic fleets. Initiatives linking ground stations and low-earth orbit satellites demonstrate the feasibility of establishing global quantum-secured communication grids, vital for cohesive military operations and strategic deterrence in an era of rapid geopolitical shifts.

Zero-Trust Architectures

Quantum keys do not operate in isolation; integrating them into modern cybersecurity paradigms is essential. Zero-trust architectures, which fundamentally assume no implicit trust within networks, benefit significantly from quantum key mechanisms. In defense networks, identity-centric frameworks use QKD-generated keys to authenticate devices, users, and services continuously, limiting lateral movement of threats and tightening access control.

Embedding quantum keys within zero-trust protocols reinforces boundary defenses with cryptographic material that is provably secure, thus elevating the fidelity of identity verification and encryption. This confluence of quantum security and zero-trust principles forms a robust barrier against insider threats, supply chain compromises, and advanced persistent threats, all while ensuring that classified information remains compartmentalized and shielded from unauthorized exposure.

Secure Voice and Video

Communications are no longer solely text-based; real-time voice and video transmissions have become critical in diplomatic dialogues and battlefield coordination. Encrypting these multimedia streams with information-theoretic security—security that does not depend on computational assumptions—adds a new layer of protection against interception and manipulation.

Quantum-derived keys enable encryption algorithms that can sustain the high bandwidths and low latency required for real-time conversations without sacrificing security. Military-grade secure conferencing thus becomes practical, where commanders and diplomats converse confidently, assured that conversations are shielded from quantum-enabled adversaries poised to break conventional cryptography. This aspect is particularly vital for coordinated responses during crises, ensuring that decision-making processes remain confidential and tamper-proof.

Cross-Domain Interoperability

Government and military communication ecosystems are complex mosaics of legacy systems, modern encrypted channels, and emerging quantum networks. Achieving interoperability—the ability to securely exchange information across these diverse architectures—is a formidable challenge. Quantum networks must bridge seamlessly with classical and post-quantum cryptographic systems to avoid creating isolated communication silos.

Strategies such as quantum key relay nodes and hybrid cryptographic gateways enable this cross-domain functionality, allowing quantum-generated secrets to secure transmissions over standard military communication hardware. Rigorous protocol design ensures that quantum keys are compatible with legacy encryption modules and intelligence community systems, fostering unified operations. This interoperability also supports multi-agency cooperation, a necessity in joint military-civil defense and international coalitions.

Red Team Exercises

Deploying quantum-secured channels is not merely a matter of installation; ongoing validation through rigorous testing is critical. Red teams—internal groups authorized to simulate adversarial attacks—now focus on quantum-specific threat scenarios. This includes attempts to intercept quantum signals, induce device side-channel leaks, or exploit weaknesses in key management and integration processes.

Such exercises reveal vulnerabilities not apparent in theoretical models, fostering iterative improvements in hardware robustness, protocol design, and operational procedures. By simulating attack vectors unique to quantum technologies, governments can anticipate emergent risks, ensuring their communication networks maintain integrity even against future adversaries armed with quantum computing capabilities.

Policy and Governance

Securely managing and operating quantum communication networks in government contexts demands stringent policies and governance frameworks. Handling classified quantum keys commands strict controls comparable to traditional key distribution but with added complexity due to the physical quantum states involved.

Standardization of operational procedures—including secure key storage, destruction protocols, audit trails, and inter-agency information sharing—is essential to maintain trustworthiness and prevent insider threats. International agreements and national regulations also guide ethical usage and export controls, balancing technological advancement with geopolitical stability and non-proliferation norms.

Field Trials

To transform quantum communication concepts into operational realities, governments have launched diverse field trials across challenging environments. Naval vessels equipped with QKD terminals experiment with secure communications across open seas; air bases integrate quantum links for real-time command exchange; and forward operating areas deploy portable quantum key devices to establish secure local networks.

These trials evaluate not only performance and reliability under extreme conditions but also the logistical and tactical implications of deploying quantum systems in military scenarios. Feedback from such programs informs design refinements, operational doctrines, and cost-benefit analyses, shaping the roadmap toward wider quantum-hardened communication infrastructure.

Quantum-secure communication thus occupies an expanding frontier in safeguarding the flow of critical information. By embedding principles of quantum physics into government and military networking—from embassies to battlefields, satellites to secure conferencing—states fortify their strategic and tactical capacities against an uncertain technological future. This quantum leap in secure messaging promises to redefine the balance of power in diplomacy and defense, embodying the fusion of scientific innovation with geopolitical necessity.

7.4 Industrial and Smart Infrastructure

The backbone of modern civilization—power grids, factories, water systems, and transport networks—depends increasingly on digital coordination and remote control. These critical infrastructures, once largely mechanical or analog, have converged with smart technologies and the Internet of Things (IoT), creating vast interconnected ecosystems that both enhance efficiency and amplify vulnerability. As adversaries grow more sophisticated, safeguarding these systems demands revolutionary security approaches. Quantum networking technologies, especially quantum key distribution (QKD), offer a promising path to robust protection—reinforcing the industrial and smart infrastructure at its most foundational levels.

At the heart of many energy and utility systems lie Supervisory Control and Data Acquisition (SCADA) networks. These systems monitor and control power generation, distribution, and metering with single-second precision. However, they are all too often vulnerable to cyberattacks aiming to alter control commands or falsify sensor data. Smart meters relay usage statistics to utilities for dynamic billing and

load management, but the data they transmit can be
tampered with or intercepted unless properly secured.
Quantum technologies empower this protection by
delivering encryption keys whose secrecy is guaranteed
by the laws of physics themselves. By integrating QKD
into SCADA communications, the integrity of control
signals and meter data can be assured, dramatically
reducing the risk of tampering or eavesdropping that
traditional cryptography might fail to detect. This
enhancement not only protects consumer information
but also safeguards grid stability, preventing potential
cascading failures triggered by malicious interference.

Beyond the utility grid, the rise of Industry 4.0 has
transformed factories into complex smart environments,
where robotic systems, automated pipelines, and
sensor arrays collaborate in near-perfect harmony.
The data exchanges facilitating robotic control and
process automation are prime targets for hackers
seeking to disrupt operations or steal intellectual
property. Deploying quantum-backed links in
these manufacturing settings establishes a secure
communication layer that resists interception, sabotage,
and insider threats. With QKD providing fresh
cryptographic keys at frequencies tailored to factory
cadence, even intercepted messages become useless
without the quantum-secure keys. This quantum
underpinning is crucial when milliseconds can affect
not just productivity but workplace safety and expensive
equipment integrity, distancing smart factories from
vulnerabilities inherent in conventional network
security.

The sprawling web of IoT devices powering smart
infrastructure—from environmental sensors monitoring
air quality to actuators adjusting valve positions—
presents a notorious challenge for authentication.

Ensuring that each device genuinely belongs to the network and that its messages are trustworthy is vital to prevent impersonation or malicious takeover. Quantum key distribution offers a pathway to create unforgeable trust anchors in these sensor and actuator networks. Rather than relying on static credentials or computational assumptions, QKD enables devices to generate shared keys intrinsically linked to quantum phenomena. This strong authentication foundation helps prevent spoofing attacks and fosters trustworthy machine-to-machine communication, encouraging wider deployment of IoT in safety-critical contexts where security concerns had previously delayed adoption.

Securing telemetry data throughout the supply chain is another crucial application. Modern supply chains extend across continents and rely heavily on sensor data to verify location, condition, and authenticity of goods. Counterfeit products or tampered shipments not only cause financial losses but can pose serious health and safety risks. Quantum-secured telemetry channels ensure the provenance and integrity of supply chain information, creating an unbroken chain of trust from manufacturing to delivery. By protecting each data handoff with quantum encryption, the system detects any unauthorized data alteration or interception attempts immediately, enhancing transparency and accountability in global logistics and certification processes.

Cyber threats do not only endanger data but can trigger physical consequences in critical infrastructure systems—water treatment plants, transportation hubs, or electrical substations must maintain systemic resilience. Combating cyber-physical threats requires an approach that integrates quantum-secured

205

communication, real-time monitoring, and fail-safe protocols. Quantum networks provide trusted communication pipelines to disseminate security updates, anomaly alerts, and control instructions without fear of interception or tampering. This protected communication fabric strengthens the infrastructure's ability to resist, isolate, and recover from attacks or failures by ensuring command integrity and timely response coordination. As a result, essential services experience fewer disruptions and improve public safety and confidence.

An emerging application area is the connectivity between physical assets and their digital counterparts— so-called digital twins. These virtual models, continuously synchronized with real-world conditions, enable predictive maintenance, optimization, and scenario analysis. The fidelity of a digital twin depends on secure and real-time data flows to prevent manipulation that could distort decision-making. Quantum-secured links guard this synchronization, ensuring that updates flowing from sensors to digital replicas, and from simulation outputs back to control systems, remain untampered. This secure bridge bolsters trust not only between machines and models but also between human operators and automation systems, fostering deeper integration of digital twins into critical infrastructure management.

This secure connectivity also expands beyond the edge into cloud ecosystems where analytics, control algorithms, and large-scale coordination take place. Combining local quantum links at infrastructure nodes with cloud-based services creates a hybrid security model: sensitive operations happen near the source with QKD-encrypted channels, while data aggregation and higher-level processing leverage quantum-secured pathways to the cloud. This edge-to-cloud integration helps balance latency, scalability, and security, ensuring that critical infrastructure harnesses the full power of modern computation without compromising confidentiality or resilience.

Despite vast potential, deploying quantum communication infrastructure in industrial environments faces significant challenges. Harsh physical conditions, such as electromagnetic interference, temperature extremes, and vibrations, require robust quantum hardware designed for rugged operation. Legacy systems must be integrated gracefully to avoid costly replacements, demanding adaptable and interoperable solutions. Maintenance and calibration of quantum networks in decentralized and often remote settings call for new skill sets and operational frameworks. Addressing these hurdles requires close collaboration between quantum technology providers, infrastructure operators, and standards bodies to build pragmatic deployment roadmaps.

Promisingly, several pilot projects highlight the practical feasibility and advantages of quantum networking in industrial settings. Industry consortia have demonstrated QKD's use in smart city testbeds, securing sensor arrays for energy, traffic, and public safety systems. Experimental smart factories showcase quantum-secured control links between robotic workstations, while power utilities have trialed QKD to protect grid data and communications. These initiatives not only validate technical concepts but also offer crucial insights into user experience, interoperability, and cost-benefit trade-offs, catalyzing wider adoption and iterative innovation.

Quantum technologies are poised to reshape the security landscape of industrial and smart infrastructure. By reinforcing the trust boundaries around critical systems,

they reduce the attack surface available to adversaries
and raise the cost and complexity of illicit access beyond
current capabilities. As IoT ecosystems proliferate
and infrastructures become more deeply intertwined
with digital intelligence, quantum networking emerges
not as a futuristic luxury but as an essential pillar for
resilient, trustworthy operation. The drive toward
quantum-hardened industrial systems marks a pivotal
moment—one where fundamental physics meets
practical engineering to protect society's most vital
foundations.

7.5 Quantum Internet for Education and Science

The quantum Internet is poised not just to revolutionize
communication technology, but to redefine how
education and scientific research unfold in an
increasingly interconnected world. By leveraging the
extraordinary principles of quantum mechanics—such
as entanglement and quantum key distribution—
quantum networks offer unparalleled security and
unique collaborative opportunities. These capabilities
empower institutions, educators, and researchers to
share knowledge, experiment remotely, and immerse
learners in the quantum realm like never before.

At the heart of this transformation is *global research
collaboration*. Traditional collaborations often grapple
with the challenges of securely sharing vast datasets
or proprietary findings across international borders.
Quantum networks promise to change this narrative by
enabling inherently secure links between universities
and laboratories worldwide. For instance, researchers
studying quantum materials or complex biological
systems generate bulky and sensitive data. Through

quantum key distribution protocols, these data can be transmitted with virtually unbreakable encryption, ensuring confidentiality and trust among collaborators. This safeguards intellectual property while accelerating scientific progress through seamless, cross-border data exchange.

Building upon secure data sharing, quantum networks facilitate the emergence of *remote and virtual quantum laboratories*, where students and scientists can perform experiments without physically being in the same space—or even the same continent. Traditionally, access to cutting-edge quantum hardware has been limited by high costs and geographic constraints. Quantum-enabled remote labs break down these barriers by using high-fidelity quantum links allowing users to control real quantum devices from afar. Such platforms elevate learning from passive observation to active experimentation, empowering students to explore phenomena like superposition and entanglement firsthand. Moreover, researchers can test new quantum algorithms or protocols collaboratively in real time, dramatically lowering the barriers to participation and innovation.

Concurrent with remote experimentation is the need for *secure educational content*. Quantum coursework—ranging from lecture materials to sophisticated software tools—represents valuable educational assets. Protecting these resources from unauthorized access or tampering is critical, especially when intellectual property or exam integrity is at stake. Quantum networks inherently support this protection through quantum cryptography techniques that can detect eavesdropping attempts and secure transmission of content with provable security guarantees. Consequently, educators gain confidence

that their curriculum remains intact and that students
interact with authentic, untampered resources, thereby
preserving academic standards.

Another exciting frontier enabled by quantum Internet
connectivity is the development of *collaborative
simulation platforms*. Quantum computers and quantum
network simulators housed in cloud environments
allow teams of students and researchers to model
complex quantum systems, optimize algorithmic
parameters, or visualize entanglement structures
simultaneously. These platforms turn collaboration into
a dynamic, interactive experience rather than a series
of disconnected efforts. Participants can share insights
instantaneously, debug code collectively, and analyze
results together, nurturing a culture of cooperation that
is critical for tackling real-world scientific challenges
that span multiple disciplines and institutions.

The advent of these cutting-edge tools necessitates
equally innovative *training and certification programs*.
Hands-on experience is essential for professionals
aiming to bridge the gap between quantum theory and
practice.   Quantum Internet emulators and testbeds
offer realistic environments where learners can simulate
quantum networking scenarios, deploy quantum
encryption schemes, and troubleshoot quantum
hardware interactions without the need for costly
physical equipment.   Educational institutions and
industry partners are already crafting programs that
leverage these testbeds, fostering a new generation
of quantum-savvy engineers, policymakers, and
educators who are well-prepared to drive the
technology's advancement while addressing its practical
complexities.

Beyond technical expertise, the profound societal
implications of the quantum Internet call for inclusive

dialogue and interdisciplinary approaches. *Interdisciplinary workshops* are emerging as vital forums where quantum technologists, social scientists, ethicists, and policymakers convene to discuss questions of privacy, access, governance, and ethical deployment. These gatherings ensure that the technology's benefits are realized responsibly and equitably, shaping frameworks that harmonize innovation with broader human values. Such collaborative discourse enriches scientific inquiry by contextualizing its impact within societal dynamics, preparing learners and researchers to navigate a technology that is as much social as it is scientific.

This ecosystem will not flourish without robust *infrastructure and access models*. To that end, university-industry partnerships are pioneering campus-scale quantum network deployments, bridging the gap between theoretical research and practical application. These initiatives not only provide essential testbeds for developing quantum networking technologies but also serve as living laboratories where students engage directly with the infrastructure they study. By embedding quantum networks into academic environments, institutions ensure graduates have firsthand experience with real-world quantum systems, fostering a workforce ready to innovate in academia and industry alike.

Several *case studies* exemplify the transformative potential of the quantum Internet within education and research. For instance, an international consortium of universities has piloted a quantum networking curriculum that integrates theoretical lectures with remote experimentation and secure collaborative projects. Researchers from different continents have successfully coordinated quantum key distribution experiments in real time while analyzing results

211

through a shared simulation platform. These pioneering efforts not only validate the practicality of quantum Internet applications but also illuminate best practices, challenges, and avenues for future expansion.

Crucial to sustaining such momentum is thoughtful *quantum curriculum development.* Designing structured courses that build upon foundational quantum mechanics while introducing concepts of quantum communication, network protocols, and cryptographic applications supports a scaffolded learning experience. Lab modules that include hands-on activities with remote quantum devices and simulator tools reinforce theoretical understanding with experiential learning. By integrating emerging quantum Internet concepts early in the educational pipeline, institutions nurture curiosity and equip students with the skills necessary for active participation in the quantum technology ecosystem.

In all these dimensions, the quantum Internet emerges not merely as a technological novelty, but as a catalyst for reimagining how knowledge is produced, shared, and safeguarded. It fosters a vibrant environment where education transcends geographic and disciplinary boundaries, experimental collaboration becomes secure and instantaneous, and learners encounter quantum phenomena as an immersive reality rather than a distant abstraction. As the quantum Internet matures, it holds the promise of democratizing access to the frontiers of science, enriching learning experiences, and accelerating discoveries that will shape our technological and intellectual landscape for decades to come.

7.6 Global Internet Innovation

Quantum connectivity is not merely a technological leap but the seedbed for a vibrant, complex ecosystem blending new standards, business models, and strategic collaborations. Its emergence is reshaping the global Internet landscape, driven by coordinated efforts among international consortia, innovative economic forecasts, and evolving service paradigms that respond to the unique capabilities of quantum networks.

Central to this transformation are organizations like the Quantum Internet Alliance (QIA), the European Telecommunications Standards Institute's Quantum-Safe Cryptography (ETSI QSC) group, and the International Telecommunication Union's Research Group on Quantum Information Technology (ITU-RG-QIT). These consortia spearhead critical standardization initiatives, ensuring that quantum technologies interoperate smoothly across national and technological boundaries. QIA, for instance, fosters integration of research outcomes into practical deployment strategies within Europe, aligning academic, industrial, and governmental stakeholders. Meanwhile, ETSI QSC concentrates on defining robust cryptographic protocols that remain secure against quantum-enabled threats, establishing the foundation for future-proofed communication systems. The ITU-RG-QIT adds a global dimension by facilitating dialogue on spectrum management, interface specifications, and harmonized regulatory frameworks. Together, these bodies craft a layered standards architecture—from hardware benchmarks to software protocols—that will underpin the reliable and scalable quantum Internet of tomorrow.

The economic implications of this infrastructure evolution are equally ambitious. Market analyses predict a substantial quantum networking sector, poised to reach tens of billions of dollars within the coming decade. This growth is anticipated to create hundreds of thousands of jobs worldwide, spanning research, engineering, manufacturing, and service provision. More notably, quantum networks promise to boost gross domestic product through enhanced cybersecurity in financial systems, accelerated discovery in pharmaceutical development via distributed computational resources, and optimized energy grids leveraging quantum sensors. The infusion of quantum connectivity into these domains catalyzes productivity gains that ripple across entire economies, positioning countries that invest early in quantum infrastructure to harness lasting competitive advantages.

This economic promise is mirrored in the emergence of novel service models built specifically for quantum networks. Quantum-as-a-Service (QaaS) platforms are gaining traction by offering on-demand access to quantum hardware and secure channels, effectively lowering entry barriers for enterprises and researchers. These cloud-like services allow users to lease quantum-secure communication links or perform distributed quantum computations without managing the underlying complexity. Meanwhile, secure conferencing solutions that utilize quantum key distribution enable tamper-proof, real-time collaboration across continents—a feature attractive to governments, multinational corporations, and critical infrastructure operators. Distributed quantum sensing networks add yet another layer, employing entangled sensors to deliver unprecedented precision in fields such as environmental monitoring and supply chain verification. Such services illustrate that quantum networks are not an abstract novelty but practical tools fostering new forms of digital interaction and collaboration.

However, the realization of this potential depends heavily on supportive policy and regulatory frameworks that can navigate the complex ethical, security, and geopolitical challenges quantum connectivity introduces. International treaties aimed at preventing misuse of quantum technologies parallel early arms control agreements, emphasizing transparency and trust-building. Export controls on quantum hardware components seek to prevent proliferation, while data protection laws are evolving to encompass encryption methods that quantum computers could threaten. Regulatory agencies face the dual task of enabling innovation through flexible standards while guarding against inadvertent vulnerabilities. The coordinated global governance emerging around quantum infrastructure underscores the recognition that quantum networks are not solely technical assets but strategic resources with implications for sovereignty and civil liberties.

Crucially, the quantum Internet's transformative impact will only be equitable if access extends beyond wealthy nations and large corporations. Closing the digital divide in this context involves deliberate strategies to bring quantum benefits to developing regions and underserved communities. Initiatives including technology transfer partnerships, capacity-building programs, and subsidized infrastructure investments aim to elevate global digital inclusion. For example, pilot projects exploring quantum key distribution in rural areas demonstrate how security enhancements may protect sensitive communications even where internet infrastructure today is limited. By embedding principles of openness and cooperation into the ecosystem's growth, stakeholders strive to prevent a

215

new form of digital inequality—one where quantum-
secure communications or advanced sensor networks
become privileges of the few.

Public–private partnerships (PPPs) play a pivotal
role in translating quantum Internet visions into
reality. Governments provide seed funding, regulatory
guidance, and research infrastructures that reduce risks
for private firms venturing into uncharted technological
territory. In return, industry brings agility, scale,
and market insights that accelerate prototype testing
and commercial deployment. Collaborative efforts
such as the European Quantum Flagship program
or the US National Quantum Initiative exemplify
this synergy, where academia, startups, established
corporations, and policy makers coalesce around
shared roadmaps. These partnerships nurture vibrant
innovation hubs, streamline knowledge exchange, and
catalyze workforce development, helping overcome the
technical and economic impediments that quantum
networks entail.

A clear standards roadmap is critical to coordinate
this diverse activity and signal maturity timelines for
investment and adoption. Over the next five to ten years,
milestones include specifying interoperable quantum
communication protocols, establishing hardware
interoperability benchmarks for quantum repeaters
and switches, and finalizing security certification
frameworks. Early phases concentrate on defining
modular components that can plug seamlessly
into existing telecom infrastructures, while later
stages address large-scale integration challenges
and international cross-border operability. Such an
evolutionary approach aims to avoid fragmented or
incompatible solutions, enabling a globally coherent
quantum Internet architecture.

To contextualize the myriad benefits quantum connectivity offers across sectors, it is instructive to consider a matrix of applications and associated advantages:

Sector	Security	Performance	Collaboration
Finance	Quantum-resistant encryption to protect transactions	Ultra-fast settlement via quantum networks	Distributed ledgers supporting real-time audits
Healthcare	Confidential sharing of patient data	Accelerated drug discovery through distributed simulations	Remote multi-institutional clinical trials
Energy	Secure command and control of smart grids	Enhanced measurement precision via quantum sensors	Coordinated resource management across regions
Government	Tamper-proof diplomatic communications	Rapid crisis response enabled by quantum networks	Cross-agency data sharing with provable integrity
Manufacturing	Protection of intellectual property	Optimization of supply chains using quantum algorithms	Collaborative design across global facilities

Table 7.1: Applications and benefits of quantum connectivity across sectors

Financing this ambitious transformation involves a mosaic of investment and funding models. Venture capital remains a driving force behind early-stage quantum startups, attracted by the promise of disruptive breakthroughs and scalable platforms. Corporate investment by technology giants and telecom incumbents provides scale and integration expertise, blending incremental upgrades with quantum innovations. Governments worldwide supplement these flows with targeted grants, prize competitions, and infrastructure bonds, recognizing

217

quantum connectivity as a strategic priority with
broad societal benefits. These diverse funding streams
reflect the recognition that quantum Internet evolution
is a marathon—not a sprint—requiring sustained,
multifaceted support.

The global quantum Internet ecosystem thus unfolds
as a tapestry of technical ingenuity, cooperative
frameworks, and novel business paradigms. Its
success hinges on orchestrating standards, investments,
policies, and inclusion strategies that reinforce each
other and accelerate adoption. Navigating this
complex terrain demands both visionary thinking
and practical collaboration, traits embodied by the
international consortia, public–private partnerships,
and innovative service models now emerging. As
quantum networks extend their reach, they promise not
just new connectivity but a fresh foundation for trust,
discovery, and shared prosperity in the digital age.

Chapter 8

Challenges on the Road to the Quantum Internet

Although the quantum Internet promises transformative advances in security and distributed computing, realizing a global network faces formidable obstacles. This chapter examines the technical, operational, economic, and societal challenges that must be overcome to deploy large-scale quantum networks. We first detail core hardware and channel limitations, then analyze decoherence and error-rate constraints. Next, we explore issues of scalability, standardization, and infrastructure costs. Finally, we address the legal, ethical, and workforce considerations essential for building and sustaining a robust quantum Internet.

8.1   Technical Barriers

Building a global-scale quantum network is, in many regards, akin to assembling a delicate, otherworldly puzzle. The pieces—quantum bits (qubits) and their carriers—must interact flawlessly over vast distances, yet they remain maddeningly fragile, subject to the laws of physics in ways classical networks never face. While the theoretical principles behind quantum

219

communication dazzle with promise, deploying these ideas into robust, large-scale infrastructure confronts a gauntlet of technical barriers. Understanding these fundamental hardware and channel limitations illuminates why progress in quantum networks is measured in painstaking increments rather than leaps.

Photon Loss and Attenuation

At the heart of quantum communication lies the photon, the quantum particle of light, which ferries quantum information across optical fibers and free-space channels. Unfortunately, photons do not always arrive unscathed. As they traverse fiber cables—or even the atmosphere— they collide with imperfections, impurities, and environmental influences. This leads to photon loss through a mix of absorption, scattering, and imperfect coupling between devices. Each photon lost chips away at the usable signal, limiting both the maximum distance a quantum message can travel and the rate at which secret keys can be securely established in protocols like Quantum Key Distribution (QKD).

Optical fibers, the backbone of the classical internet, have attenuation coefficients typically around 0.2 dB/km at telecom wavelengths, meaning about 5% of photons are lost per kilometer. While this seems modest, the math quickly becomes unforgiving: over 100 km, fewer than 1% of photons survive. Importantly, classical repeaters can simply amplify weakened signals to compensate, but quantum states cannot be amplified without disturbing their fragile superpositions and correlations. Hence, attenuation imposes a hard distance limit—usually less than a few hundred kilometers—for direct quantum communication without intermediate assistance.

Entanglement Distribution Limits

Quantum entanglement functions as the backbone of

many quantum network protocols, enabling correlations between distant nodes that classical physics cannot mimic. Establishing entangled photon pairs across long distances without degradation is a critical prerequisite. Yet, the same photon loss and noise that impair single-photon transmission also threaten entangled states.

In practice, direct distribution of high-fidelity entangled pairs is confined to a few hundred kilometers over optical fiber. Beyond this, noise accumulates, and the entangled pairs deteriorate into useless mixtures. This distance boundary arises from the combined effects of attenuation and imperfections in entanglement generation and detection. While satellite links can circumvent some terrestrial limits by exploiting lower atmospheric losses and line-of-sight visibility, ground-based fiber networks remain challenging, especially inside bustling, signal-rich urban infrastructures.

Quantum Repeater Complexity

To breach the distance barrier posed by photon loss, the concept of the quantum repeater emerges—an imaginative device that divides a long communication link into shorter segments. By creating and storing entanglement in each segment, and then stitching these segments together through quantum teleportation and entanglement swapping, repeaters can theoretically extend communication to continental scales.

Yet, quantum repeaters are not simple amplifiers dressed in fancy clothing. They demand complex architectures combining quantum memories, entangled photon sources, precise synchronization, and error correction. Resource-wise, these stations are substantially more demanding than classical nodes: they require stable quantum memories with long coherence times, switching networks, and often cryogenic conditions.

Designing such intricate machines, integrating their various subsystems without disturbing fragile quantum states, and scaling them reliably remains one of the grand engineering hurdles in quantum networking.

Quantum Memory Performance

Storing quantum information in a memory device long enough to perform operations like entanglement swapping is another formidable challenge. Quantum memories must retain coherence—the undisturbed quantum state—with extremely high fidelity, typically over milliseconds to seconds, depending on protocol demands.

Current quantum memories, based on trapped atoms, ions, or solid-state systems, face a trade-off between storage time, retrieval efficiency, and operational complexity. Environmental perturbations such as stray magnetic fields and temperature fluctuations cause decoherence, collapsing the stored state prematurely. Furthermore, the process of retrieving the stored qubit without introducing additional errors remains imperfect. These limitations impose bottlenecks on repeater performance and, by extension, on network reach and throughput.

Source and Detector Imperfections

Generating and detecting single photons perfectly on demand is foundational—and notoriously tricky. Photon sources, often based on nonlinear optical processes or quantum emitters like quantum dots and ions, rarely produce photons at exactly the desired time, with consistent wavelength, or with perfectly defined properties. Timing jitter—the uncertainty in photon emission and detection times—can degrade entanglement fidelity and synchronization. Similarly, detector inefficiencies and dark counts (false positives) introduce errors and reduce usable data rates.

For instance, superconducting nanowire single-photon detectors (SNSPDs) offer excellent efficiency but require cryogenic cooling and can still suffer from limited timing resolution. These non-idealities ripple through the system, complicating error correction and lowering the ultimate performance ceiling.

Cryogenic and Isolation Requirements

Quantum platforms that underpin many quantum network components—such as superconducting qubits, certain single-photon detectors, and some quantum memories—demand ultra-low temperatures, often fractions of a degree above absolute zero. Achieving and maintaining such cryogenic conditions involves complex refrigeration systems that consume significant power and introduce mechanical vibrations.

In parallel, isolating these delicate systems from environmental noise—acoustic vibrations, electromagnetic interference, temperature gradients—is essential. Even minuscule perturbations can decohere quantum states or introduce phase noise. These technical requirements restrict where and how quantum hardware can be deployed, complicating integration into the widespread, heterogeneous infrastructure of existing communication networks.

Heterogeneous Hardware Integration

Quantum networks rarely rely on a single qubit technology. Instead, they must interconnect diverse physical implementations—trapped ions, nitrogen vacancy centers in diamond, quantum dots, or atomic ensembles— each with unique advantages and operational demands. Moreover, interfacing these quantum systems with classical control electronics and optical components introduces further complexities.

223

Achieving seamless integration that preserves the delicate quantum information requires meticulous engineering. Challenges include mode matching between distinct photon wavelengths, managing differing operational temperatures, synchronizing control signals, and minimizing insertion losses at interfaces. Without mastering heterogeneous integration, large-scale networks risk becoming patchworks of incompatible segments rather than unified systems.

Synchronization and Clock Distribution

Coordinating operations across widely separated quantum nodes demands extraordinarily precise timing. Quantum protocols often rely on interference effects, entanglement swapping, or joint measurements, all of which must be synchronized to sub-nanosecond accuracy. Any drift in clocks or timing errors can reduce fidelity or cause outright protocol failure.

Classical synchronization methods such as GPS signals or fiber-based timing distribution face limitations in precision and stability. Designing dedicated quantum-compatible clock distribution systems presents a fresh frontier, requiring innovations in timing hardware, protocols, and error mitigation to maintain coherence across sprawling networks.

Environmental Sensitivity

Quantum devices are exquisitely sensitive to their surroundings. Temperature fluctuations can cause expansion or contraction of components, altering optical path lengths and phase properties. Magnetic field variations disturb spin-based qubits, leading to rapid decoherence. Mechanical stress and vibrations snag quantum states by shaking or deforming delicate structures.

Mitigation techniques exist—magnetic shielding, temperature stabilization, vibration isolation—but they add cost, complexity, and infrastructure overhead. These sensitivities illustrate why quantum systems often demand lab-like conditions, complicating their transition into the field, especially in mobile or urban environments subject to unpredictable disturbances.

The dream of a functioning quantum network stitching together the globe is daunting not because the quantum rules are inscrutable, but because the physical realities of hardware and communication channels impose stubborn constraints. Photon loss caps range; entanglement struggles to survive long distances; repeaters are architectural mountains rather than stepping stones; memories flicker before their time; and sources, detectors, and environmental stability all conspire to frustrate efforts. Each barrier reflects the delicacy of quantum information itself.

Yet these challenges are not walls but hurdles, inviting innovation in materials, engineering, and system integration. Understanding these technical barriers grounds our optimism in reality, revealing why quantum networks are among the most demanding—and fascinating—technological frontiers of the twenty-first century.

8.2 Error Rates and Quantum Decoherence

Quantum information is famously fragile, and its delicate nature poses one of the central challenges in building reliable quantum technologies. As quantum bits—or qubits—evolve and interact with their surroundings, they invariably lose the pristine quantum

states that encode information.   This degradation,
known as *decoherence*, manifests as both errors in
quantum operations and gradual loss of stored
quantum memory.   To sustain workable quantum
networks, scientists must first quantify how quantum
states deteriorate, then devise strategies to mitigate
these losses throughout processing and transmission.

At the heart of decoherence is interaction with the
environment—everything from stray electromagnetic
fields to microscopic vibrations in the substrate hosting
the qubits.   Two dominant effects arise due to these
interactions: *phase damping*, where coherence between
quantum states is scrambled, and *amplitude relaxation*,
where system energy dissipates, causing the state to
relax toward a thermal equilibrium.   Phase damping
can be imagined as the quantum bit's delicate phase
relationship becoming randomized, analogous to a
marching band gradually losing rhythm.   Amplitude
relaxation, on the other hand, corresponds to a qubit
spontaneously losing its excitation, akin to a lit bulb
slowly dimming as it consumes its energy.

Scientists characterize these effects using two fundamental timescales, known as *relaxation time* (T_1) and *dephas-
ing time* (T_2). The T_1 time quantifies how quickly a qubit
loses its energy and decays from the excited state to the
ground state—effectively how long it "remembers" its
initial population.   The T_2 time measures how long the
qubit maintains the phase coherence essential for quantum superpositions, capturing the interval before phase
randomization makes the stored quantum information
useless.   Typically, T_2 is shorter than or equal to $2T_1$, reflecting that loss of phase coherence often precedes or
accompanies energy dissipation.

These decay processes are often modeled exponentially
to describe the probability that the original quantum

state survives after a given time t. For example, the simple population decay in a two-level system can be expressed as

$$\rho(t) = \rho(0)e^{-t/T_1},$$

where $\rho(t)$ represents the state's population at time t, and $\rho(0)$ the initial state. This exponential decay elegantly captures the relentless erosion of quantum information over time, whether the qubit is stored in memory or transmitted through a communication channel.

But decoherence is hardly limited to storage; every gate operation—be it a quantum logic gate or a measurement—introduces its own flavor of imperfections. Gate errors arise from imprecise control pulses, cross-talk between qubits, and hardware imperfections, while readout errors stem from limitations in accurately measuring qubit states. Typical error rates per quantum operation currently hover between 0.1% and 1%, which, while seemingly small, accumulate rapidly as quantum circuits grow complex. Without intervention, these compounded errors cascade, corrupting outputs and undermining entire protocols.

When signals traverse long quantum links, imperfections multiply further, elevating the *quantum bit error rate* (QBER). Originating from hardware noise, photon loss, or timing jitter in optical networks, QBER measures the fraction of qubits incorrectly transmitted or decoded. Just as a whisper grows unclear when passed along a long chain of people, quantum states degrade as they cross fiber optics or free space, with noise sources continuously increasing error rates. This growth of QBER sets stringent limits on the feasible distances of quantum communication without repeaters.

To wrestle decoherence into submission, researchers

227

have developed several error mitigation techniques.

- *Dynamical decoupling* involves applying carefully timed sequences of control pulses that refocus and cancel out environmental noise, much like flipping a spinning top to compensate for wobbling.

- *Composite pulses* replace simple control operations with sequences engineered to be robust against certain errors, improving gate fidelities without additional hardware.

- *Decoherence-free subspaces* encode information in collective states immune to specific noise types, akin to secret signals inaudible to an eavesdropper.

Even with these techniques, the dream of perfectly reliable quantum operations remains out of reach due to the inherent physical limitations and engineering challenges. This is where *quantum error correction* codes enter the stage, promising fault-tolerant operation by encoding logical qubits into multiple physical qubits and actively detecting and correcting errors. However, such error correction imposes a significant overhead: a single logical qubit might require dozens or even hundreds of physical qubits, along with continuous monitoring and fast feedback, greatly increasing hardware complexity and resource consumption.

The feasibility of fault-tolerant quantum computing and communication hinges on achieving error rates below certain *thresholds*. These thresholds represent error bounds under which the benefits of error correction outweigh the costs, making reliable operation scalable. Currently, fault-tolerance thresholds are believed to lie near error rates of 10^{-3} or lower, meaning that each gate and operation must perform correctly more than 99.9%

of the time. Achieving such precise control requires an intricate dance of materials science, hardware engineering, and algorithmic design.

Error rates and decoherence also impact the overall performance trade-offs in quantum networks. Enhancing fidelity through extended error correction and mitigation reduces error accumulation but often at the cost of throughput. Complex protocols allocate time and qubit resources for error handling, reducing the effective data or key rates achievable in applications such as quantum cryptography. Optimizing this balance between fidelity and speed is a fundamental challenge still being navigated in real-world quantum systems.

Ultimately, decoherence and error rates constrain how far and how well quantum information can travel, how long it can be faithfully stored, and how complex the computations can be before noise overwhelms the signal. While error mitigation and correction offer powerful tools, each introduces new challenges and costs. Understanding and mastering these phenomena remain crucial for transforming the promise of quantum networks from laboratory curiosity into everyday reality.

8.3 Scalability and Standardization

Building a quantum network is a feat akin to assembling a delicate web that spans vast distances—but unlike classical networks, it must tightly weave together the fragile threads of quantum states. As these networks stretch beyond laboratories and into commercial, governmental, and even global domains, two intertwined challenges come to the forefront: *scalability* and *standardization*. Only by tackling both can

229

the vision of a functional quantum Internet come to fruition.

Network Scaling Challenges

Scaling quantum networks is not simply about adding more nodes or extending connections indefinitely. Each quantum link—whether a fiber optic channel carrying single photons or a satellite-based quantum downlink—suffers from loss and noise that increase dramatically with distance. Unlike classical signals that can be amplified at will, quantum information cannot be cloned or boosted without compromising its delicate quantum properties. Hence, increasing the number of nodes and stretching link lengths introduces exponential difficulties in maintaining quantum fidelity and key transmission rates.

Classical networks thrive on robust signal regeneration and buffering, but quantum mechanics imposes a different reality. With longer distances, photon losses multiply, and noise accumulates. This forces network architects to innovate solutions that circumvent or mitigate these effects rather than simply increasing hardware amounts. Furthermore, the physical resources required—such as quantum memories, single-photon detectors, and entangled photon sources—do not scale linearly. Carefully balancing cost, performance, and complexity becomes paramount.

Repeater Placement Strategies

Quantum repeaters are the backbone technology envisioned to extend the range of quantum communication. They perform the demanding task of entanglement swapping and purification, effectively stitching shorter, higher-fidelity links into longer, usable chains. However, determining where and how many repeaters to place is a nuanced exercise in optimization.

Placing repeaters too sparsely risks losing fidelity and reducing key rates to impractical levels; overcrowding them inflates costs and operational complexity beyond necessity. Strategies for repeater placement weigh factors such as the physical environment (urban versus rural terrain), attenuation of the quantum channel, and desired security guarantees. Models often incorporate probabilistic analyses showing how link success rates, memory lifetimes, and error correction overhead interplay to define an optimal density.

For example, in metropolitan quantum networks aiming for secure citywide links, repeaters might be densely packed every few kilometers. In contrast, continental-scale or satellite-integrated networks require far fewer ground stations but with more sophisticated quantum memory and error correction capabilities. Developing frameworks that incorporate these trade-offs lays the groundwork for scalable, practical deployments.

Hardware Interface Standards

Interoperability begins at the physical layer. Quantum nodes and repeaters manufactured by different companies or research labs must ultimately speak a common language in terms of electrical, optical, and timing signals. Without agreed-upon hardware interface standards, integrating devices risks becoming a Gordian knot of incompatible connectors, pulse formats, and clock frequencies.

These standards encompass the shape and wavelength of photons used, synchronization protocols that ensure distant nodes' clocks align to the nanosecond, and the electrical signals governing control electronics. Achieving this across a rapidly evolving landscape of hardware—ranging from trapped ion systems to solid-state memory arrays—is a Herculean but essential

231

task.

Well-defined interfaces foster modularity and competition, accelerating innovation while ensuring a swap-in, swap-out ability that classical networks take for granted. Moreover, they reduce the cost of network maintenance and upgrades by preventing vendor lock-in.

Protocol Interoperability

Once hardware speaks the same language, higher-level dialogue must also be standardized through common protocols. Quantum networks rely on an intricate choreography of message exchanges: directing entanglement generation, confirming link status, error detection, and recovery, all while preserving the quantum state's integrity.

Standardizing message formats, handshake procedures, and control application programming interfaces (APIs) is critical to avoid fragmentation—a proliferation of isolated quantum islands unable to share resources or extend services. Protocols dictate how disparate network elements negotiate, establish trust, and orchestrate the elusive quantum dance of entanglement distribution.

Initiatives in this direction borrow lessons from decades of classical network protocol design but adapt them creatively due to the fundamentally different properties of quantum information. For example, a classical acknowledgment packet confirming receipt cannot be mimicked directly; instead, quantum-specific methods like heralding signals—conditional notifications triggered by successful quantum operations—carry similar roles. Defining these protocols openly enables third-party developers and network operators to innovate atop a stable foundation.

Performance and Security Benchmarks

Without agreed-upon metrics, assessing and comparing quantum network components or configurations would be like setting off on a journey without reliable maps. Performance benchmarks must quantify key operational parameters such as secret key generation rates, fidelity of entangled states, latency in establishing links, and overall network reliability.

Moreover, security benchmarks scrutinize how well a system resists eavesdropping attempts, environmental noise, and hardware imperfections. Quantum networks promise inherently secure communication, but this promise depends on rigorous standards that verify security claims under realistic conditions.

Uniform metrics allow users and regulators to evaluate products, foster competition on measurable grounds, and guide research priorities. They also provide essential feedback loops during network scaling, helping pinpoint bottlenecks and validating improvements.

Standards Bodies and Consortia

Crafting standards in any emerging technology involves collaboration and sometimes contention between stakeholders with varied interests. The quantum networking arena is no exception. Several international standards bodies and consortia have stepped forward to define norms, facilitate interoperability, and build consensus frameworks.

Organizations such as the International Telecommunication Union (ITU), the European Telecommunications Standards Institute (ETSI), and the Institute of Electrical and Electronics Engineers (IEEE) bring decades of telecommunications standardization expertise to bear. More specialized alliances, like the Quantum Internet Alliance and Quantum Industry Canada, focus on the unique demands of quantum technologies.

233

These entities convene experts from academia, industry, and government to balance innovation pace with the need for stable, widely compatible standards. Their work includes publishing technical reports, conducting interoperability workshops, and managing open testbed networks. Active participation in these forums ensures that standards reflect the latest scientific breakthroughs while remaining grounded in practical deployment realities.

Testbed Interconnection

Prototyping quantum networks in isolated labs offers proof-of-concept insights, but validating scalability and interoperability demands linking regional testbeds into larger ecosystems. Interconnecting different testbeds—each possibly employing distinct hardware and software—demonstrates whether cross-domain quantum communication protocols and interfaces hold up beyond controlled environments.

These federated testbeds serve as real-world laboratories where developers confront unforeseen latency issues, synchronization challenges, and unexpected noise sources. Success here builds confidence that future multinational quantum networks will not be fragmented into incompatible silos.

Examples include linking metropolitan quantum networks across cities and countries, or connecting satellite-ground nodes with terrestrial fiber-based testbeds. Each interconnection venture uncovers critical lessons, from hardware compatibility to network management strategies, driving standards refinement and architectural evolution.

Software Control Layer Standards

Beneath the sleek user-facing applications lies a complex

software stack managing the orchestration of quantum resources. The control layer interfaces between the quantum hardware on one side and network management services and applications on the other. Standardizing *northbound* APIs (towards applications) and *southbound* APIs (towards hardware) is fundamental to building modular, scalable systems.

This separation enables software developers to write applications and orchestration algorithms without intimate hardware knowledge while allowing hardware vendors to improve devices independently from higher-level controls. For instance, a northbound API may expose services like entanglement reservation, key negotiation, or network state monitoring, while southbound protocols translate these requests into pulse sequences or memory management commands.

Clear semantic definitions of control messages, error reporting formats, and feedback loops underpin efficient debugging, automated network adaptation, and secure operation. Open software standards also encourage community contributions and accelerate innovation cycles.

Global Addressing and Routing Frameworks

A fully realized quantum network calls for robust schemes to name devices, discover available resources, and route entanglement across multiple network domains. Unlike classical packets that are copied and forwarded, quantum information must be transmitted with minimal disturbance, often necessitating intricate entanglement swapping and path selection algorithms.

Designing a global addressing system is a nontrivial task, requiring considerations of security, scalability, and privacy. Naming conventions must provide unique, persistent identifiers for quantum devices and channels, en-

abling discovery services that react in real time to link
failures or fluctuating performance.

Routing frameworks decide which paths entanglement
should traverse, balancing overall network efficiency
and local resource constraints. These routing protocols
may integrate quantum-aware heuristics such as path
fidelity estimation and resource reservation, differing
substantially from classical counterparts.

Establishing these frameworks lays the groundwork for
an agile, adaptable quantum Internet capable of spanning continents and connecting heterogeneous networks
seamlessly.

Key Requirements and Initiatives for Scaling and Stan-
dardizing Quantum Networks

The grand challenge of expanding quantum networks
beyond experimental setups into everyday infrastructure hinges on a dual imperative: achieving scalable
architectures while fostering comprehensive standards.
Addressing fundamental physical limitations through
intelligent repeater designs and placement strategies
goes hand in hand with creating open, interoperable
frameworks for hardware, protocols, and software.

Standardized interfaces—both physical and logical—
unlock vendor diversity and competition, while
rigorous benchmarks ensure transparent comparison
and reliability. Collaborative efforts by standards bodies
and testbed federations forge consensus and validate
the building blocks across technical and organizational
boundaries.

Only through this coordinated attention to scalability
and standardization will the quantum Internet
transcend its laboratory origins, unlocking its full
promise as a transformative global communication

paradigm.

8.4 Cost, Infrastructure, and Accessibility

Deploying quantum links—the core arteries of the emerging quantum Internet—invites a complex mix of economic and logistical challenges. These challenges are not merely a byproduct of pioneering new technology; they stem from the intrinsic demands of quantum systems, which fundamentally differ from classical networks. Understanding the financial and infrastructural landscape is crucial to grasping where quantum communication stands today and the path it must carve toward widespread adoption.

At the heart of the capital expenditure lies an intricate constellation of components and installations. Fiber-optic cables still form the backbone of many quantum links, but unlike traditional fibers, quantum fibers need exceptionally low-loss characteristics and often require deployment along meticulously planned routes. Laying new fiber is notoriously costly, involving labor-intensive trenching, right-of-way negotiations, and protective housing. Beyond the fiber itself, specialized hardware pushes costs upward. Cryogenic equipment—essential for cooling quantum devices such as superconducting detectors or certain quantum memories to millikelvin temperatures—consumes a significant portion of startup budgets. These refrigeration systems are not only power-hungry but require continuous maintenance to maintain their ultra-low temperatures. Detectors capable of registering single photons with high efficiency and low noise represent another significant investment. Finally, satellites equipped for quantum key distribution and entanglement distribution offer tantalizing possibilities

237

for global reach, but launching and maintaining space-borne quantum devices remain an expensive frontier.

Operational expenses add another layer of complexity. Running quantum links is not a "set and forget" affair. Maintenance teams must regularly calibrate delicate quantum components to account for environmental drift, fiber aging, and hardware variability. Calibrations often involve precision lasers and timing equipment that necessitate expert oversight. Power consumption for cryogenic systems and associated electronics is substantial, demanding robust energy supply infrastructures with redundancy to ensure continual uptime. Perhaps less tangible but equally critical are the costs of specialized personnel. Quantum engineers, optical technicians, and quantum information scientists command premium rates, reflective of their rare expertise. Training and retaining such staff further strain operational budgets.

These economic factors manifest visibly in the network's physical footprint. Quantum nodes and repeaters do not simply fit into existing telecom closets; they require dedicated spaces with controlled environments to ensure stability. Temperature and vibration regulation, electromagnetic shielding, and clean-room conditions may all be necessary to prevent decoherence and maintain quantum state fidelity. This level of environmental control inflates costs and complicates site selection, especially in dense urban areas or regions lacking advanced facilities. Power requirements—both for cryogenics and active electronics—demand infrastructure often beyond standard networking equipment, influencing design decisions from the outset.

For smaller players—academic research labs, startups, and organizations in emerging economies—the threshold for joining quantum networks remains daunting. Initial capital requirements and ongoing costs can be prohibitive. Without economies of scale or access to public funding, these groups face substantial barriers to entry, risking a two-tiered landscape where quantum technologies serve primarily well-funded entities. The broader vision of a quantum Internet relies on democratized access, making this disparity a pressing concern.

Innovative funding solutions have emerged to address these challenges. Public-private cost-sharing models, often in the form of consortia or government-backed testbeds, reduce financial burdens by pooling resources and distributing risk. Collaborative frameworks allow partners to share expensive infrastructure investments such as metropolitan fiber loops, satellite links, or cryogenic facilities. These consortia perform a dual function: accelerating technology deployment and fostering communities of practice that spread expertise and standardize protocols. Such partnerships also facilitate funding mechanisms that balance private investment with public interest, creating pathways for sustainable growth.

Phased roll-out strategies further align deployment with real-world constraints. Rather than betting everything on full-scale networks from the outset, incremental expansions—starting with metropolitan demonstration networks, followed by regional and then intercontinental links—help control risk and spread expenditures over time. These staged approaches allow for iterative learning, gradual technology maturation, and budget adaptability. Early successes can prove business cases, inviting more private and governmental investment, thereby catalyzing subsequent phases.

Complementing phased deployment is the development

of open access testbeds. These shared facilities, often located within research institutions or innovation hubs, lower entry barriers significantly. By providing remote or on-site access to quantum networking equipment, they empower smaller organizations and international collaborators to experiment without the need for massive upfront capital. Testbeds serve as incubation grounds for novel applications and foster a culture of transparency and collective problem-solving that benefits the entire ecosystem.

As hardware matures and production scales, economies of scale are expected to exert a transformative effect on costs. Like many high-tech fields—from classical computing to photovoltaics—unit costs of quantum components are projected to decline steeply once manufacturing transitions from artisanal prototype crafting to automated assembly lines. Such scaling applies to photon detectors, cryogenic coolers, integrated photonic chips, and satellite payloads alike. Moreover, standardized interfaces and modular designs will reduce integration complexity, streamlining maintenance and training overheads.

Nonetheless, robust business cases remain a prerequisite for widespread adoption. Quantifying return on investment requires not only accounting for upfront and operational costs, but also estimating the value quantum networks can unlock. These include enhanced cybersecurity through quantum key distribution, new communication paradigms leveraging entanglement for distributed quantum computing, and robust timing services. Business models are still evolving, with some focus on secure government communications and financial services, while others explore hybrid classical-quantum solutions. Clear demonstrations of cost-effectiveness, scalability, and unique features will be decisive in motivating enterprises and governments to shift resources toward quantum infrastructure.

Navigating through cost, infrastructure, and accessibility conditions reveals a technology poised between promise and financial reality. Quantum networks demand substantial resource commitments and meticulous planning, both to build and to operate. Yet collaborative innovation, sensible roll-outs, and technological maturation promise to ease these burdens gradually. The true challenge lies in orchestrating these pieces—economic, engineering, and social—so that quantum links evolve from niche experiments into accessible, reliable pillars of a future Internet.

8.5 Legal and Ethical Considerations

As quantum networks transition from theory to practical reality, they present a compelling frontier not only in technology but also in law, policy, and ethics. The unprecedented capabilities of quantum communication—chiefly its promise of unbreakable encryption—raise complex questions that challenge existing legal frameworks and social norms. Addressing these concerns now is essential for harnessing quantum networks responsibly and inclusively.

One of the most challenging dilemmas involves *data sovereignty and jurisdiction*. Quantum networks can span continents, linking users across borders with cryptographic keys generated through quantum key distribution (QKD). These keys and the encrypted data they protect do not adhere to national boundaries. Under traditional legal frameworks, data hosted or routed through different countries fall under their respective laws—privacy regimes, data retention

241

requirements, and surveillance powers often vary widely. Quantum networks complicate this because the physical transmission of quantum states may be intangible or indirect, making it difficult to determine which laws apply. For example, if a key is generated in one jurisdiction but used to decrypt sensitive information in another, it remains unclear which legal protections govern the process. This uncertainty necessitates new international agreements explicitly addressing cross-border quantum information flows, balancing national interests with users' rights.

Closely related to data sovereignty are *export controls and national security* concerns. Quantum hardware— such as photon sources, delicate detectors, or satellites enabling QKD—are often dual-use technologies. While advancing scientific knowledge and secure communications, the same devices could enable adversaries or upset global strategic balances if proliferated indiscriminately. Governments have long imposed export restrictions on sensitive cryptographic tools, and quantum technologies now entering their prime are becoming part of this restrictive regime. Satellite-based QKD, for instance, presents unique challenges: the satellite's hardware or firmware can be transferred, hacked, or otherwise compromised, and its orbital path traverses multiple national territories. Regulating these technologies without stifling innovation or collaboration remains contentious. International dialogue, transparent licensing, and trust-building among states offer a potential path forward, but the tension between openness and security will intensify as quantum capabilities mature.

Another regulatory frontier is *spectrum and frequency allocation*. Quantum signals transmitted through free space, such as ground-to-satellite or terrestrial line-of-sight QKD, must coexist with classical wireless communication on crowded electromagnetic bands. Although quantum communications often operate in optical frequencies less congested than radio bands, allocation and interference concerns echo those in traditional telecommunications. Quantum channels require high fidelity and low noise; even minor disruptions can compromise delicate quantum states. Regulatory bodies face the challenge of balancing quantum users' need for protected frequencies with the growing demands of conventional spectrum users such as mobile networks, broadcasting, and emergency services. Coordinated spectrum management, integrating the unique sensitivities of quantum communications, is crucial to prevent harmful interference and ensure reliable operation.

The deployment of quantum networks also raises important questions regarding *liability and incident response*. What are the implications if a quantum link suffers an outage at a critical moment—potentially severing secure communications during a cyberattack? If a breach occurs, even if classical data security is preserved because of quantum encryption, could vulnerabilities in key management or hardware failures create backdoors? Assigning responsibility for such failures is complex. Quantum technologies involve multiple parties: hardware manufacturers, network operators, service providers, and end users. Liability frameworks must evolve to clarify accountability for outages, data loss, or unintended disclosure. Moreover, incident response protocols require updating to address quantum-specific risks, including detecting and mitigating attacks on quantum states and swiftly restoring secure links. Transparency in incident reporting and clear mechanisms for redress are essential

243

to build user trust and encourage broader adoption.

Central to ethical quantum network deployment are *user privacy rights*. Quantum encryption's primary appeal lies in its theoretically unparalleled security, promising to protect individuals' communications from eavesdroppers, including state actors. However, security alone does not guarantee ethical use. Transparency about how quantum data is generated, transmitted, and stored is vital for informed consent. Users must understand what quantum security entails for their privacy and recognize any limitations or residual risks. For example, if quantum keys are generated but stored insecurely at endpoints vulnerable to classical hacking, privacy can still be compromised. Ethical guidelines should require openness about such realities, empowering users to make informed decisions. Furthermore, quantum networks should be designed with privacy-by-design principles, minimizing unnecessary data collection and ensuring robust safeguards.

Beyond individual rights, *equitable access and the digital divide* require urgent attention. Early quantum Internet services may disproportionately benefit wealthy nations, research institutions, or large corporations, potentially exacerbating existing inequalities in technological access. Ensuring that secure communications, enhanced cybersecurity, and new quantum-enabled applications are widely and fairly accessible demands proactive policy measures. These may include subsidizing infrastructure development in underserved regions, promoting open standards, and fostering international partnerships. Without deliberate effort, the quantum Internet risks becoming yet another frontier of digital exclusion, deepening social and economic divides. Broader inclusion will also accelerate innovation by diversifying the community of users and stakeholders.

The dual-use nature of quantum communications introduces complex *risks of misuse*. While quantum networks promise robust security, they may also enable malicious actors to communicate covertly, spreading disinformation or coordinating illicit activities with near-perfect secrecy. Moreover, quantum-resistant cryptographic techniques could disrupt law enforcement capabilities if deployed without safeguards. Thoughtful policies must navigate these risks by establishing legal boundaries and monitoring mechanisms that deter misuse without stifling legitimate privacy or innovation. The enduring debate regarding encryption backdoors—a perennial issue in classical cryptography—is certain to reemerge in quantum contexts, necessitating nuanced balancing of security, privacy, and public safety.

Addressing these multifaceted challenges requires the development of *governance frameworks* tailored specifically to quantum networks. Multi-stakeholder models involving governments, industry, academia, and civil society offer promising approaches to develop norms, standards, and enforcement mechanisms. Such frameworks should integrate technical expertise with ethical perspectives and legal analysis, fostering international cooperation and harmonization. Examples include global bodies similar to the International Telecommunication Union or the Internet Governance Forum, convening to address quantum-specific issues, facilitating dialogue, and reducing fragmentation. Effective governance must be adaptive, transparent, and inclusive to keep pace with the rapid evolution of quantum technologies.

These legal and ethical considerations form the foundation upon which trustworthy and socially responsible quantum networks will be built. They

245

underscore that technological breakthroughs alone
cannot guarantee a better future; rather, the interplay of
law, policy, and ethics will determine whether quantum
communications serve the public good or introduce new
vulnerabilities. Navigating this landscape demands
collaborative commitment to safeguarding fundamental
rights, fostering innovation, and ensuring equitable
access—so that the immense promise of quantum
networks becomes a shared reality.

8.6 Education and Workforce Skills

As the promise of a quantum Internet inches closer
to reality, one essential ingredient stands out: the
human factor. Building, operating, and advancing
such a revolutionary network depends heavily on a
workforce equipped with a distinctive blend of skills
and knowledge. Unlike classical networks, which have
matured over decades of conventional engineering
and computer science education, the quantum Internet
demands a new breed of expertise—one that straddles
quantum physics, cutting-edge engineering, and
advanced information theory. Cultivating this talent
pool requires deliberate strategies spanning education,
training, and professional development.

At its core, the quantum Internet workforce must pos-
sess nuanced skillsets that reflect the novel challenges of
quantum technologies. Quantum physics forms the theoretical backbone; a firm grasp of principles like superposition, entanglement, and quantum error correction
is fundamental. Concurrently, engineering know-how
is critical, especially in designing and maintaining delicate hardware such as quantum repeaters and photon
detectors. Network systems knowledge completes the
triad, enabling professionals to understand routing pro-

tocols, security architectures, and integration with classical infrastructure. This interplay means that the workforce cannot be siloed but must develop fluency across domains, ensuring practical fluency alongside conceptual comprehension.

Meeting these demands begins within the educational ecosystem. Curriculum development in universities and technical institutes is shifting to embrace hybrid programs that weave together quantum theory, experimental labs, and software training tailored for quantum network operations. Traditional physics courses are complemented by hands-on modules focusing on photonics, cryogenics, and quantum algorithms. Simultaneously, software components introduce students to quantum programming languages and network simulators. This interdisciplinary approach provides learners with a tangible grasp of both the abstract mechanics and real-world applications of quantum communication. Furthermore, embedding capstone projects and internships fosters problem-solving skills and industry readiness—a pivot from passive knowledge acquisition toward active engineering and innovation.

Certification pathways are emerging as another vital pillar, shaping a clear professional identity for quantum network engineers and operators. Professional certifications, akin to classical networking credentials but honed for quantum contexts, serve multiple purposes. They standardize competence benchmarks, facilitate trust among employers, and encourage continual learning in a rapidly evolving field. Organizations are beginning to collaborate on credentialing frameworks that validate expertise in quantum cryptography, network design, and operational protocols. Such credentials also help distinguish specialists in a crowded technology landscape, easing workforce mobility and career progression. Importantly, these certifications do not replace formal education but augment it by attesting to hands-on skills and up-to-date knowledge.

The gap between academia and industry, a perennial challenge in emerging fields, is particularly acute here due to the quantum Internet's novelty and complexity. Recognizing this, many institutions and companies have forged partnerships that blend research, teaching, and workforce cultivation. Joint programs enable students to engage with real-world problems through internships, co-developed courses, and research collaborations, ensuring that graduates emerge with relevant experience and insights. Industry partners benefit from early access to fresh talent and innovative ideas, while academia gains valuable feedback to iterate curricula. Such symbiotic relationships accelerate the maturation of quantum networking technologies and smooth the transition from theory to practice.

Yet the path forward also involves those currently entrenched in classical IT domains who aspire to pivot into quantum roles. Workforce transition programs are essential to equip these professionals with foundational quantum knowledge alongside practical skills in quantum device handling and network configuration. Retraining initiatives may take the form of intensive boot camps, online courses, or hybrid instruction formats tailored to adult learners balancing existing careers. By building bridges rather than erecting barriers, these programs mitigate workforce shortages and facilitate the infusion of experienced personnel into the quantum ecosystem, addressing the pressing demand for capable quantum Internet practitioners.

A truly sustainable and innovative quantum workforce

must also reflect the broad diversity of society. Diversity and inclusion initiatives aim to ensure that underrepresented groups—be it by gender, ethnicity, socioeconomic background, or geography—have equitable access to quantum education and career opportunities. Broadening participation is not merely a fairness mandate; diverse teams have repeatedly demonstrated creative problem-solving and robust outcomes across scientific and technological frontiers. Scholarship programs, mentorship networks, and targeted outreach efforts help dismantle systemic barriers, cultivating a vibrant talent pool whose varied perspectives can drive breakthroughs in quantum networking and beyond.

Equipping learners extends beyond theoretical study. Hands-on experience is indispensable, gained through access to testbeds and simulators that replicate quantum Internet environments on manageable scales. Shared experimental platforms allow students, researchers, and developers to experiment with quantum hardware and software in controlled settings, explore network protocols under varied conditions, and innovate new solutions with immediate feedback. Software emulators provide a complementary avenue, simulating quantum network behaviors where physical apparatus remains scarce or costly. These experiential resources accelerate learning curves, reduce abstractness, and stimulate creative exploration, ultimately grounding education in the realities of quantum communication.

Scaling these educational efforts globally requires embracing the digital age. Online and remote learning platforms expand reach, making cutting-edge quantum Internet instruction accessible irrespective of geographic constraints. Massive open online courses (MOOCs), virtual labs, and interactive tutorials cater to a global audience, allowing flexible pacing and personalized engagement. This democratization of knowledge is particularly crucial for emerging economies and regions without established quantum infrastructure, enabling participation in the global quantum revolution. Moreover, digital communities foster collaboration, peer support, and knowledge exchange, shaping a distributed yet connected ecosystem of learners and practitioners.

Finally, the multidisciplinary nature of quantum Internet development calls for interdisciplinary collaboration as a cornerstone of workforce formation. Bridging computer science, physics, engineering, and even social sciences enriches understanding and innovation, addressing not only technical challenges but also economic, ethical, and societal implications. Training programs are evolving to incorporate this broad perspective, encouraging teams to navigate the complexities of quantum security policy, user experience, and regulatory frameworks alongside technical design. Such holistic workforce development ensures that quantum Internet deployment is not just a technological feat but a thoughtfully integrated societal advancement.

Taken together, these strategies form a coherent framework for cultivating the human capital vital to a quantum Internet future. By defining and nurturing essential skillsets, innovating educational pathways, aligning academia with industry needs, and promoting inclusivity and practical engagement, the ecosystem sets the stage for sustained growth and innovation. As quantum networks progress from laboratory curiosities to foundational infrastructure, the strength and agility of the workforce will determine how fully society can harness their transformative potential.

Chapter 9

Looking Ahead: The Future of Quantum Internet

In this concluding chapter, we chart the evolution of quantum networking from today's prototypes toward a fully realized global quantum Internet. We first highlight emerging research breakthroughs and technological trends, then examine the major international initiatives and partnerships shaping standards and large-scale deployment. Next, we present expert predictions and milestone timelines for the coming decades, followed by actionable strategies for organizations to prepare for quantum-driven disruption. Finally, we reflect on the ethical and societal implications of ubiquitous quantum connectivity and provide concrete steps for readers to get involved in this unfolding frontier.

9.1 Research Trends and Innovations

As quantum networks evolve from intriguing laboratory curiosities to practical communication frameworks, a wave of scientific and technological advances is driving the field to new horizons. The challenges of transmitting fragile quantum information over long distances and through noisy environments have spurred innovations that promise to reshape the architecture, scale, and efficiency of future quantum networks. These emerging trends, each addressing a crucial bottleneck or offering novel capabilities, collectively advance the dream of a robust, global quantum internet.

One foundational leap is *integrated photonics*, which replaces bulky, discrete optical components with monolithic chip-scale circuits. Much like microelectronics transformed computing by scaling down transistors into compact chips, integrated photonic platforms enable thousands of low-loss waveguides, switches, and detectors on a single silicon or lithium niobate wafer. This miniaturization not only slashes signal attenuation but also facilitates scalable multiplexing: routing multiple quantum signals simultaneously within a compact footprint. The consequence is a leap in complexity and portability, allowing quantum nodes to become more practical and cost-effective for real-world deployment.

Complementing advances in hardware, *advanced repeater protocols* aim to extend the reach of quantum communication. Traditional quantum repeaters, which relay entangled states to bridge long distances, face limitations from imperfect memories and photon loss. Newer schemes exploit multiplexing techniques—sending many quantum signals in parallel across distinct frequency or temporal modes—and integrate quantum error correction methods to actively detect and repair errors before they accumulate. These protocols reduce the classical latency and resource overhead that previously restricted repeater performance, potentially enabling entanglement distribution across continental scales with high fidelity.

Pushing the capacity of quantum channels further, *high-dimensional quantum key distribution (QKD) techniques* seek to encode multiple bits of information in a single photon by exploiting properties beyond polarization or simple binary states. Notably, photons possessing orbital angular momentum (OAM)—twisted light beams shaped like tiny optical vortices—can carry a theoretically unbounded set of orthogonal states. Likewise, encoding information simultaneously in time and frequency dimensions offers a rich alphabet without increasing photon count. By packing more information per photon, these methods enhance bandwidth and security, proving particularly promising for urban quantum networks where channel capacity is at a premium.

Underlying many of these active transmission strategies are quantum memories, whose experimental sophistication is rapidly improving. *Multimode quantum memories* represent a critical breakthrough by enabling the storage of multiple quantum bits or temporal modes simultaneously. Rather than a single quantum state captured at a time, these memories act like multiplexed warehouses, holding many entangled states until successful synchronization across the network is possible. This capability is pivotal for scaling quantum repeaters and supporting high-throughput quantum communication, akin to having a multitasking brain rather than a single-thread processor.

All these technologies hinge on maintaining quantum coherence and mitigating errors, a challenge that has inspired notable progress in *error-correction breakthroughs*. New families of quantum error-correcting codes, optimized for realistic hardware constraints, have emerged to dramatically reduce the overhead of physical resources needed to encode and protect quantum information. Additionally, novel architectures incorporate fault-tolerant designs where error detection

253

and correction are embedded within the network nodes themselves, rather than relying solely on classical post-processing. This integration points toward robust quantum communication systems that can operate reliably even in imperfect, noisy environments.

Meanwhile, a complementary direction addresses the complexity of managing quantum networks at a systemic level. Inspired by classical networking, *quantum network stack models* introduce layered frameworks that delineate responsibilities across physical, link, and application layers. Such models provide a common language and blueprint to design interoperable protocols, enabling quantum devices from different labs or companies to communicate seamlessly. By defining these layers—analogous to the TCP/IP stack in the classical internet—researchers and engineers can modularize development, foster standards, and accelerate adoption.

Bridging the gap between existing infrastructure and emerging quantum technology, *hybrid classical–quantum architectures* propose software-defined approaches that integrate quantum links into conventional communication networks. These architectures leverage programmable control layers to dynamically allocate resources and route quantum signals alongside classical data, optimizing network usage without requiring fully quantum-only systems. This hybridization facilitates a gradual, practical rollout of quantum capabilities, allowing incremental upgrades rather than wholesale replacements.

Extending the reach of terrestrial quantum networks beyond line-of-sight limitations, *satellite and aerial platforms* are gaining prominence. Recent developments in small-satellite constellations specifically designed for quantum missions, along with unmanned aerial vehicles (UAVs) equipped with quantum nodes, promise to deliver entanglement and secure keys across regions where fiber optic or ground-based links are impractical. These airborne and orbital relays may soon form a space-based backbone for global quantum communication, dramatically increasing coverage and connecting isolated nodes on Earth.

Scaling from proof-of-concept systems to meaningful deployments requires robust infrastructure development plans. Researchers are developing *testbed scaling strategies* to transition from single-node laboratories to city-wide or campus-scale multi-node quantum networks. These strategies focus on modularity, fault tolerance, and ease of expansion, along with comprehensive benchmarking of real-world performance under environmental and operational variability. Such testbeds not only validate technologies but also provide invaluable data to refine protocols and hardware for commercial readiness.

Finally, as the field matures, *collaborative simulation frameworks* have become instrumental in accelerating innovation. Researchers worldwide are contributing to shared computational toolchains for modeling quantum network components, simulating protocols at scale, benchmarking performance, and openly exchanging experimental data. This collaborative ecosystem minimizes duplication of efforts, encourages reproducibility, and helps build consensus on promising architectures and standards, catalyzing community-wide progress.

Together, these trends weave a vivid tapestry of progress and promise. Each breakthrough—whether in materials, protocols, architectures, or collaboration—complements the others, addressing the intricate interplay of physics, engineering, and information science that defines quantum networking. As these innovations coalesce, the vision of an interconnected quantum web, capable of secure communication, distributed computing, and new forms of sensing, moves steadily closer to reality. The coming decade could witness quantum networks transitioning from niche applications to pervasive infrastructure, redefining not only how we communicate but also the very fabric of information itself.

9.2 Global Initiatives and Collaborations

The quest to realize a fully operational quantum Internet is no longer confined to isolated laboratories or singular nations; rather, it has become a grand, multinational endeavor. This transformation owes much to a constellation of national programs, international consortia, pilot infrastructures, and a rich tapestry of collaborations that span continents and cross political boundaries. These coordinated efforts not only expedite technological progress but also weave together a global fabric of quantum communication that promises unprecedented security and connectivity.

Many countries have recognized quantum technologies as strategic priorities, launching ambitious national programs that act as production lines for innovation as well as beacons attracting international partners. Prominent among these is the United States National Quantum Initiative (NQI), established in 2018 with comprehensive funding and a mandate to accelerate research across quantum sensing, computing, and networking. The NQI integrates efforts from government agencies, national laboratories, academia, and industry, creating a symbiotic ecosystem fostering breakthroughs. Meanwhile, the European Union's

Quantum Flagship is a decade-long, multi-billion-euro initiative coordinating over a hundred research projects to build a competitive quantum technological base across member states. Both programs emphasize the quantum Internet as a cornerstone for secure communications and distributed quantum computing. China has likewise invested heavily in quantum communications, pioneering quantum key distribution (QKD) networks that span metropolitan areas and even connecting multiple cities with fiber links and satellite channels, culminating in one of the world's largest quantum communication infrastructures.

Beyond national ambitions, international consortia are essential orchestrators of collaboration, governance, and standardization. The Quantum Internet Alliance (QIA), funded by the EU, exemplifies an effort to combine scientific excellence with engineering prowess, pulling together universities and companies from several countries to develop foundational quantum networking technologies. On the standards front, bodies such as the European Telecommunications Standards Institute's Quantum-Safe Cryptography group (ETSI QSC) and the International Telecommunication Union's Quantum Information Technology Group (ITU-RG-QIT) work tirelessly to create interoperable protocols and certification frameworks that will ensure devices and networks can work seamlessly across borders. These organizations confront one of the quantum Internet's more formidable challenges: harmonizing diverse hardware, software, and security models into a coherent global system.

Perhaps the most tangible symbol of quantum collaboration is the European Quantum Communication Infrastructure (EuroQCI) pilot project. EuroQCI aims to link quantum-safe communication nodes across

EU member states via a hybrid quantum backbone, integrating ground-based fiber optics with satellite links. This network will underpin critical applications such as government communications, emergency services, and financial transactions with near-perfect cryptographic security. By constructing this scalable pilot, Europe seeks not only technological leadership but also policy coherence, fostering trust among nations and industries reliant on the highest assurances of privacy.

Moving to the Asia-Pacific region, a vibrant ecosystem of metropolitan testbeds accelerates real-world quantum networking demonstrations. Singapore, Japan, and Australia have built collaborative urban networks where universities, research centers, and telecom operators experiment with QKD systems, entanglement distribution, and quantum repeaters. These testbeds showcase the viability of integrating quantum links into existing telecommunications infrastructure, preparing the region for widespread commercial rollouts. By engaging multiple stakeholders—from academic researchers to private sector engineers—these testbeds dissolve traditional barriers and cultivate innovation driven by immediate practical insights.

Satellite-based quantum key distribution has emerged as another frontier uniting global initiatives. China's *Micius* satellite, launched in 2016, stunned the scientific community by distributing quantum keys securely over thousands of kilometers, including between continents. This free-space communication circumvented the distance limitations of fiber optics and opened the high ground for quantum networks. Following *Micius*, projects such as *Q-Voyager* from the US and several commercial ventures are crafting next-generation satellites aimed at creating a global quantum mesh.

These aerial platforms promise not only secure communication but also a backbone for future quantum computing clouds spanning continents, thereby knitting together national networks into a planet-wide quantum Internet.

Public–private partnerships have become a vital engine powering these diverse initiatives. Governments supply funding, regulatory frameworks, and strategic oversight, while telecom operators and technology companies contribute infrastructure, market insights, and engineering talent. Such collaborations shorten the path from research to deployment by aligning incentives and sharing risks. For instance, in the US, firms specializing in quantum hardware partner with federal agencies invested in national security, ensuring their technologies meet real-world demands within appropriately regulated environments. Europe and Asia follow similar models, where consortia include small startups alongside global telecom giants, creating competitive yet cooperative ecosystems.

Universities and academic research networks also hold an indispensable role in this complex landscape. Consortia of leading universities—from Delft in the Netherlands to the University of Tokyo and Australian National University—develop open-access quantum backbones that serve as foundational scientific testbeds. These networks allow researchers worldwide to conduct experiments on entanglement distribution, quantum routing, and error correction in authentic multi-node configurations. The resulting knowledge flows freely between academia and industry, providing a wellspring of innovation and educating the next generation of quantum engineers.

Cross-border pilot projects further refine the technical and regulatory complexities of a global quantum Inter-

net. Fiber-optic trials linking countries such as Germany
and France, or Singapore and Malaysia, test interoperability between differing quantum hardware and protocols under varying legal jurisdictions. These pilots address issues from timing synchronization to data privacy
laws, forging blueprints for future multinational quantum service agreements. Their successes help allay concerns that quantum networks are hampered by geopolitical fragmentation, instead representing potential vectors
for closer international cooperation.

Establishing clear and universally accepted standards
remains essential for the quantum Internet's maturation. Various standards working groups develop
specifications that cover messaging formats, hardware
interfaces, quantum-safe cryptographic algorithms,
and network management protocols. These efforts
are crucial not only to enable diverse technologies to
communicate effectively but also to build confidence
among users and regulators. Without shared definitions
and certification schemes, the quantum Internet risks
becoming a patchwork of incompatible islands rather
than a unified global system.

Finally, knowledge-sharing forums, including international conferences, workshops, and online communities,
act as intellectual meeting grounds where ideas, results,
and challenges circulate openly. Events such as the
International Conference on Quantum Communications,
Measurement and Computing (QCMC) bring together
scientists, engineers, policymakers, and entrepreneurs
to debate progress and shape future directions. Online
platforms further democratize access to cutting-
edge research and foster dynamic collaborations
unconstrained by geography.

Together, these national programs, consortia, infrastructures, testbeds, satellite campaigns, partnerships,

research networks, pilot links, standards, and forums form a synergistic web accelerating the quantum Internet from a tantalizing vision to an unfolding reality. The intricate dance of public and private, academic and industrial, local and international actors exemplifies how the future of secure communication and distributed quantum computing depends not on isolated brilliance but on collaborative ingenuity spanning the globe.

9.3 Predictions for the Next Decades

The quantum Internet, once confined to theoretical papers and laboratory curiosities, is steadily transitioning into an engineering reality. Expert forecasts, drawn from both ongoing experiments and visionary roadmaps, paint a dynamic picture of its emergence over the coming decades. These predictions relate not only to technological breakthroughs but also to evolving applications and market transformations. To make sense of this trajectory, it helps to consider the development in temporal layers: short-term foundations, medium-term expansion, and long-term maturity.

In the short term—roughly the next five years—the focus gravitates towards establishing robust, metropolitan-scale quantum key distribution (QKD) networks. These city-sized testbeds leverage fiber optic cables interlaced with quantum devices to enable ultra-secure communication links. Early repeater prototypes, which aim to extend the reach of entangled photons beyond current distance limitations, are being integrated into these networks. This milestone represents a crucial proof-of-concept, showing that quantum information can be reliably generated, managed, and distributed in existing urban infrastructures. For instance, cities such as Beijing, Geneva, and Tokyo have already begun deploying QKD systems safeguarding financial and governmental communications. These deployments not only validate the technology but also generate invaluable data to drive refinements.

Moving forward, the medium term—spanning approximately 10 to 15 years—envisions quantum backbones stretching across continental scales. Here, interoperable networks formed by linking metropolitan clusters will emerge, setting the stage for a quantum Internet that surpasses isolated demonstrations. The maturation of quantum repeaters, both novel and fully functional, will transform current hubs into nodes within a cohesive fabric. This period also marks the advent of nascent quantum cloud services, wherein users remotely access quantum processors and specialized algorithms over quantum-secured channels. Such services, initially adopted by research institutions and security agencies, hint at the scalable potential of quantum networks far beyond experimental setups. As a practical illustration, multiple countries have publicly committed to developing continental quantum backbones, recognizing that such infrastructure underpins future competitive edge in data security and scientific collaboration.

In the more distant horizon of 20 or more years, the outlook broadens considerably. The quantum Internet is expected to be truly global, knitting together continents with quantum links that surpass classical limitations. At this juncture, routine, widespread secure communication becomes just one facet of the network's utility. The other transformative feature is the seamless support for distributed quantum computing— multiple quantum processors interconnected to dramatically expand computational power and resource accessibility. This global network could empower scientific simulations, optimization problems, and cryptography at levels unattainable today. We might witness cloud services where quantum algorithms operate on distributed nodes, collaborating across the planet in real time, underpinned by unprecedented security guarantees.

Timeframe	Milestone	Geographic Scale / Application
Next 5 years	Metro-scale QKD deployments	Cities, financial and governmental networks
	Early quantum repeater prototypes	Extension of link distances beyond 100 km
10–15 years	Continental quantum backbones	Interconnected metropolitan networks
	Interoperable quantum networks	Cross-border collaborations and standards
	Quantum cloud services begin	Remote quantum computing for research
20+ years	Global quantum Internet	Worldwide secure communication and computing
	Distributed quantum computing	Collaborative algorithms across distant nodes
	Commercial quantum broadband	Widespread access and integration with classical Internet

Table 9.1: Key predicted milestones for the quantum Internet development over the next decades.

The trajectory of use cases follows a similarly layered evolution. Early applications emphasize secure messaging, leveraging quantum properties to foil eavesdroppers definitively—a leap beyond classical encryption's reliance on computational complexity. With time, applications will diversify and deepen. Quantum-enhanced sensing will emerge, using entanglement to refine measurements in navigation, medical imaging, and environmental monitoring. Later

still, distributed quantum computing will redefine
problem-solving paradigms, integrating quantum
algorithms into logistics, pharmaceuticals, and artificial
intelligence. For example, a quantum sensor network
could detect subtle earthquakes or atmospheric shifts
undetectable by classical instruments, while distributed
quantum AI systems might optimally manage energy
grids or autonomous vehicles with unparalleled
efficiency.

This progression, however, does not exist in isolation
from classical networks. The future quantum Internet
will not replace today's digital infrastructure but will
rather converge with it. Architects foresee unified
systems where traditional packet-switched routing
coexists with entanglement-based quantum routing.
Such hybrid architectures will allow seamless transitions
between classical and quantum data flows, ensuring
compatibility and broader accessibility. For instance, a
user sending a confidential quantum key might traverse
quantum nodes where possible, falling back on classical
encryption otherwise—much like how mobile devices
switch between Wi-Fi and cellular networks today. This
convergence reduces barriers to adoption and smooths
the transition, fostering a hybrid ecosystem enriched by
the strengths of both worlds.

Market and industry landscapes are poised for
substantial shifts as quantum Internet technologies
mature. Telecommunications providers anticipate
new service categories, from quantum-secured virtual
private networks to on-demand quantum computing
resources. Revenue models will evolve accordingly,
potentially resembling cloud computing's subscription
plans but incorporating quantum-specific instruments
such as entanglement-as-a-service. Cybersecurity
firms will pivot towards quantum resilience, offering

tools that safeguard classical and quantum data alike. Early adopters in finance, defense, and pharmaceuticals, sectors with stringent confidentiality and computational intensity, will likely spearhead demand before broader consumer markets emerge. This economic reshaping will cascade, prompting new standards, regulatory frameworks, and ecosystem partnerships, collectively accelerating innovation.

Behind these milestones and market trends lies a pattern familiar to new technologies: the *S-curve* of adoption and maturity. Initial excitement triggers a rapid learning and deployment phase, characterized by experimental pilot projects and prototype rollouts. This often meets a plateau, reflecting the considerable technical and infrastructure challenges still to be overcome. Eventually, breakthroughs and economies of scale catalyze a surge of widespread adoption, driving down costs and sparking novel use models. With the quantum Internet, these curves may be steeper— given the accelerating pace of quantum hardware development—yet they are also subject to unique pitfalls, such as coherence times and entanglement swapping fidelity. Understanding these adoption dynamics helps stakeholders gauge readiness and set realistic expectations.

Taken together, these expert predictions sketch an intricate, unfolding story. The coming decades will witness quantum networks move from constrained experiments to integrated urban fabrics, then link vast regions with quantum backbones, and finally blossom into a truly global quantum Internet. Each phase brings not only incremental gains but profound qualitative shifts—in technologies, applications, and markets. These milestones will define key inflection points where quantum communication leaves the lab and enters

everyday life, reshaping how information is shared,
protected, and processed on a planetary scale.

9.4 Preparing for Disruption

The arrival of quantum networking promises to reshape
the way organizations connect, communicate, and safeguard information. Yet, this quantum leap is less a sud-
den revolution and more a complex evolution—one that
demands advance planning. Organizations eager to capitalize on its benefits and sidestep its risks must cultivate strategic foresight, practical preparation, and adaptive resilience. The foundation of this readiness lies in a
suite of targeted actions that together smooth the pathway from current classical networks towards a hybrid
and eventually fully quantum-enabled infrastructure.

Central to any preparation is a rigorous *quantum
risk assessment*.   Unlike conventional cybersecurity
evaluations that focus solely on today's threats,
quantum risk assessment must peer into the near
future, gauging vulnerabilities exposed by quantum
algorithms and quantum-enabled eavesdropping. For
example, classical public-key cryptosystems, which
safeguard much of today's secure communication,
stand vulnerable to Shor's algorithm running on a
sufficiently powerful quantum computer. Establishing
this assessment involves cataloging assets—data,
hardware, protocols—and mapping how quantum
capabilities might compromise them. The complexity
arises in balancing current security investments against
quantum risk timelines, which remain uncertain. Yet,
this anticipatory analysis is crucial: organizations
that understand their quantum exposure early can
prioritize resources, accelerate cryptographic upgrades,
or institute interim quantum-resilient measures like

post-quantum cryptography.

With an informed risk profile, the next step is *roadmap development*—a phased blueprint charting how an organization will pilot, scale, and ultimately integrate quantum networking technologies. This roadmap typically initiates with targeted pilot projects, testing quantum key distribution (QKD) links or entanglement-based network components in controlled environments. Such pilot testbeds enable hands-on learning and operational calibration without disrupting production systems. Subsequent phases involve incremental scaling, fostering hybrid networks that meld classical and quantum links, before full integration. Thoughtful roadmap design considers timing, technical milestones, vendor maturity, and budget constraints, aligning quantum adoption with broader organizational goals. Crucially, it serves as a communication tool, rallying stakeholders across departments and articulating realistic expectations about quantum networking's transformative—but gradual—trajectory.

The technological and operational complexity of quantum networking also underscores the importance of *standards engagement*. As multiple competing approaches and protocols emerge—from quantum key distribution standards to quantum internet protocols—organizations must actively participate in standards bodies and industry consortia. This involvement helps ensure their architecture aligns with evolving consensus, gaining interoperability and future-proofing investments. Beyond technical alignment, contributing to standards development empowers organizations to influence policy, guide regulatory frameworks, and avoid being passive recipients of prescriptive rules. For instance, involvement in groups like the Internet Engineering Task Force's Quantum Internet

Research Group (IETF QIRG) or the International Telecommunication Union's Focus Group on Quantum Information Technology positions organizations both to learn from peers and to help shape the standards governing quantum networking's unfolding future.

No roadmap can succeed without people equipped to navigate the quantum landscape. Organizations must institute *workforce training plans* that build quantum literacy and cultivate specialized skills. This goes beyond simple awareness sessions; it requires developing teams conversant in quantum principles, aware of quantum threats and opportunities, and proficient with emerging tools and protocols. Training often intersects with recruiting new talent from physics, computer science, and engineering disciplines familiar with quantum technologies. Moreover, fostering a culture of continuous learning is vital, given the rapid evolution of the field. Practical methods include targeted workshops, partnerships with academic institutions, and hands-on experience within testbed environments—giving staff the confidence to innovate responsibly and respond flexibly as quantum networks roll out.

Complementing human capital investment is the deliberate design of *hybrid networks*—systems architected from the outset for seamless interoperability between classical and quantum components. Since quantum networking is unlikely to replace classical infrastructure wholesale in the near term, hybrid architectures serve as a practical bridge. For instance, deploying quantum key distribution atop existing fiber optic backbones requires sophisticated integration layers that manage both quantum-generated keys and classical data streams. Designing these architectures thoughtfully minimizes bottlenecks and enables gradual technology infusion. It also facilitates fallback options, where classical systems supply baseline connectivity while quantum elements add enhanced security or new functionalities. In this vein, hybrid design embodies pragmatic resilience, recognizing the transitional nature of quantum networking deployment.

Of course, transformation requires resources, bringing *investment and budgeting* considerations to the forefront. Quantum networking entails spending on research, equipment procurement, pilot deployments, and staff training—each with uncertain timelines and returns. Establishing dedicated budgets signals organizational commitment and ensures funding continuity amidst competing priorities. Some organizations allocate portions of their innovation budgets specifically for quantum initiatives, treating them as long-term strategic bets rather than short-term projects. Furthermore, partnerships with governmental programs or consortia can catalyze investment efficiency—sharing costs, risks, and knowledge. By proactively budgeting, organizations avoid the scramble for funds down the line and position themselves as early movers in the quantum era.

Navigating this emerging landscape also demands *regulatory compliance alignment*. As quantum networks evolve, policymakers worldwide grapple with questions about data sovereignty, cryptographic standards, and critical infrastructure security. Organizations that proactively engage with regulators and industry groups gain early insight into potential rules and can influence their formulation to balance innovation with security. This engagement might include contributing to consultations, participating in regulatory sandboxes, or collaborating on pilot projects sanctioned by authorities. Aligning compliance strategies with anticipated

quantum regulations mitigates the risk of future
retroactive constraints or costly remediation efforts,
smoothing the integration of quantum networking into
existing operational and legal frameworks.

Pilot projects serve as crucial proving grounds for all
these preparatory efforts. Establishing *pilot testbed
deployments*—whether internal facilities or collaborative
platforms shared with partners—allows organizations
to experiment with quantum networking components
under realistic conditions.   These testbeds reveal
practical challenges of hardware integration, signal
loss management, and protocol synchronization.
They also cultivate cross-disciplinary teamwork,
merging the expertise of quantum physicists, network
engineers, and security specialists.   Lessons learned
from testbeds inform roadmap adjustments, training
refinement, and investment decisions.   As quantum
technologies mature, these pilot environments become
indispensable laboratories for innovation, risk reduction,
and confidence-building.

Underlying the technical and organizational changes
needed is the human dimension of *change management*.
Introducing quantum networking technologies demands not just new tools, but new mindsets, workflows,
and collaborations.   Resistance, uncertainty, and
knowledge gaps are natural obstacles. Effective change
management involves transparent communication—
clarifying why quantum networking matters and how
it differs from classical paradigms.   It also calls for
involving stakeholders early, addressing concerns,
celebrating milestones, and fostering champions
who advocate for quantum readiness within the
organization. By embedding flexibility and adaptability
into processes, organizations create cultures poised
to absorb technological disruption rather than be

overwhelmed by it.

Preparing for the quantum networking revolution is therefore a multifaceted endeavor. Organizations must rigorously assess risks, architect well-sequenced roadmaps, engage actively in standards evolution, build quantum-capable teams, craft hybrid infrastructures, secure funding, align with emerging regulations, deploy pilots, and manage cultural shifts. Viewed holistically, these steps transform quantum networking from an abstract possibility into a tangible, manageable journey. They provide a compass not only to survive quantum disruption but to harness it—setting the stage for a future where the entanglement of technology and strategy yields unprecedented connectivity and security.

9.5 Ethical Implications of Ubiquitous Quantum Networking

As quantum networking advances from theoretical possibility to everyday reality, it invites a profound reckoning not only with new technologies but with the values that will underpin our interconnected future. The transformative promise of near-instantaneous, ultra-secure quantum communication provokes both exhilaration and unease. It is crucial to anticipate and unpack the ethical and societal challenges that will accompany the pervasive rollout of quantum connectivity.

Privacy versus Surveillance

Quantum networks are lauded for their inherent security advantages, chiefly quantum key distribution, which underpins unbreakable encryption. This could redefine digital privacy, thwarting hackers and protecting

271

sensitive information with unprecedented rigor. Yet, this enhanced security comes with a paradox. The very infrastructure enabling bulletproof communication can also be co-opted for unparalleled surveillance capabilities. Governments and corporations might exploit quantum sensors and entangled state monitoring to observe behaviors and communications with little possibility of evasion. The tension lies in balancing the empowerment that privacy affords individuals against the creeping risk of a surveillance state amplified by quantum tools. Ensuring that privacy protections keep pace with technical advances requires thoughtful legal frameworks recognizing both the promise and peril embedded in quantum networks.

Digital Divide Risks

While the quantum Internet promises to propel some regions and communities into a new era of connectivity and computational power, there is a stark risk of exacerbating global inequalities. The infrastructure for quantum networking—specialized hardware, fiber optic links intertwined with quantum repeaters, and quantum satellites—is costly and complex, likely concentrated initially in wealthy nations and urban centers. Without deliberate policy interventions, marginalized populations and developing countries may find themselves cut off from the advantages quantum connectivity offers, from secure communications to advanced AI applications powered by quantum-enhanced data. This digital divide risks deepening existing social fractures—not only economically, but also through unequal access to emerging education, healthcare, and governance platforms built atop quantum networks. Closing this gap will require global cooperation and inclusive investment strategies to democratize quantum access.

Dual-Use and Misuse Potential

Quantum networking's dual-use nature demands sober reflection. Like many groundbreaking tools throughout history, its benefits coexist with the potential for misuse. Authoritarian regimes could exploit quantum links to consolidate power, deploying quantum-enhanced surveillance to stifle dissent with chilling efficiency. Militaries might pursue quantum network-based weapons or disruptive capabilities, ushering in a new arms race that blends cyberspace and quantum physics. Meanwhile, criminal enterprises could harness quantum encryption to outmaneuver law enforcement, complicating efforts to combat illicit activities. Restraining these threats calls for international agreements and export controls, as well as interdisciplinary dialogue to anticipate misuse scenarios and develop countermeasures before crises emerge.

Algorithmic Fairness

Quantum networks will not stand apart from the data ecosystems they propagate; they will accelerate and enrich them. Quantum-enhanced analytics and artificial intelligence systems will draw on these connections for superior problem-solving or pattern recognition. However, this leap in capability may amplify existing biases embedded in data or algorithm design. If quantum-powered decision-making tools are trained on flawed or incomplete datasets, their reach and impact could magnify injustices, eroding trust and fairness in areas as critical as criminal justice, hiring, or resource distribution. Ethical stewardship demands rigorous examination of algorithmic fairness, accompanied by transparency, accountability, and ongoing impact assessment to ensure quantum technologies serve inclusive and equitable ends.

Environmental Sustainability

The material and energy demands of mounting quantum hardware networks warrant careful scrutiny. Quantum devices often rely on cryogenic cooling, exotic materials, and precise fabrication techniques with nontrivial environmental footprints. Scaling quantum communication infrastructure to global levels could consume considerable resources and energy, challenging the sustainability goals crucial to our century. As quantum technologies mature, it will be indispensable to innovate not only for performance but for ecological responsibility, optimizing designs for energy efficiency and recyclable components. Sustainable deployment models are no longer optional but imperative if quantum networking is to thrive in harmony with planetary health.

Governance and Accountability

The complex ecosystem of quantum networking implicates myriad actors: technology developers, governments, service providers, and end-users. Establishing clear governance frameworks is essential to delineate responsibilities, rights, and oversight mechanisms. Transparency in decision-making and accountability for ethical lapses must be built into the very fabric of quantum Internet institutions. The experience of classical Internet governance offers lessons—both cautionary and instructive—in balancing innovation with public interest. Creating flexible, inclusive governance models that adapt to rapid technological shifts while embedding ethical norms will help prevent power imbalances and foster user trust.

Informed Consent Models

Quantum networking introduces subtle challenges for user autonomy and informed consent. Given the inherent complexity and novelty of quantum communications, individuals may struggle to understand how their data is managed, the nature of quantum-enabled services, or the risks involved. Traditional models of consent—opaque user agreements or bundled opt-ins—will fall short in an environment where quantum protocols dynamically interact with data streams in ways previously unimagined. Designing clear, accessible consent mechanisms that genuinely empower users to make voluntary and informed choices about quantum connectivity is paramount. Opt-in policies, ongoing user education, and transparency about data use will be critical pillars supporting ethical quantum Internet adoption.

Ethical Standards Development

To navigate the uncharted ethical terrain of quantum networking, establishing widely recognized codes of conduct and best practices is vital. Stakeholders must collaboratively develop these standards, drawing on interdisciplinary expertise that blends physics, computer science, ethics, and social science. Such standards should address issues from privacy safeguards to equitable access, from responsible innovation to environmental stewardship. Proactively crafting these guidelines can help normalize behavior consistent with societal values before problematic patterns become entrenched. International cooperation and public-private partnerships will play key roles in promoting adoption and enforcement, embedding ethics as a core tenet of quantum Internet progress.

Public Engagement and Education

The societal stakes of ubiquitous quantum networking call for active public engagement. Quantum technology's unfamiliarity and complexity can breed

misconceptions, fear, or disengagement unless
addressed through inclusive dialogue. Educational
initiatives must demystify quantum concepts and
illuminate the potential benefits and risks in a language
accessible to all. Engaging diverse communities—
beyond technologists and policymakers—fosters
social license and empowers people to participate in
shaping the quantum Internet's trajectory. Democratic
participation helps avoid techno-optimism blind spots
and ensures a richer ethical vision that respects plurality
and collective well-being.

Ethical Evolution of the Quantum Internet

Charting the ethical course for ubiquitous quantum networking involves integrating these considerations into a
cohesive framework. Privacy must be fiercely protected
without enabling unchecked surveillance. Equity in access must be prioritized to prevent new digital divides.
Vigilance against dual-use threats and algorithmic bias
must be institutionalized. Environmental impacts must
be minimized alongside technical innovation. Transparent governance, robust consent models, and the development of global ethical standards, buoyed by meaningful public participation, form the pillars of a just quantum Internet future. Navigating this frontier demands
not only scientific ingenuity but also moral imagination—
anticipating not just what quantum networks can do, but
what they ought to do for humanity.

9.6 How to Get Involved

Embarking on a journey into the quantum Internet
ecosystem offers a unique blend of scientific discovery,
technological innovation, and collaborative opportunity.
This emerging domain is not reserved solely for

physicists or computer scientists; enthusiasts, technologists, and curious minds from diverse backgrounds can contribute meaningfully. The quantum Internet promises to reshape communication and computation, and your pathway into this frontier can be shaped by education, hands-on experimentation, community engagement, and more. Here, we explore a suite of accessible resources and initiatives designed to welcome newcomers and seasoned professionals alike, empowering you to help steer the future of a truly quantum-connected world.

Educational Programs and Certifications

Building a solid foundation is essential, and fortunately, numerous educational opportunities cater to diverse levels of expertise and commitment. Leading universities across the globe now offer specialized courses in quantum information science, quantum computing, and quantum networking. For instance, programs at institutions such as MIT, Stanford, and the University of Oxford provide rigorous coursework that blends theory with emerging applications. Beyond physical campuses, Massive Open Online Courses (MOOCs) like those found on edX, Coursera, and Quantum University present flexible options to grasp quantum fundamentals and their networked applications.

In parallel, professional certifications have begun to appear, often offered by industry consortia and research alliances. These credentials validate knowledge in quantum networking protocols, security aspects, and even hardware operation, serving both newcomers eager to establish competence and experienced practitioners seeking formal recognition. Together, these educational pathways create a scaffold that guides aspirants from curiosity to expertise, ensuring the quantum Internet's architects are well-prepared to solve its complex challenges.

Simulation Sandboxes

Since direct access to quantum networks remains limited and expensive, simulation environments are invaluable for experimental learning and development. Platforms like IBM's Qiskit, NetSquid, and QuTiP offer robust frameworks to design, test, and refine quantum communication protocols in a virtual setting. Qiskit, for example, started as a quantum computing platform but now includes modules geared toward simulating networked quantum systems. NetSquid focuses explicitly on simulating quantum networks, enabling users to model photon transmission, entanglement distribution, and error correction techniques with remarkable fidelity.

QuTiP, while often associated with quantum dynamics and control, supports the exploration of qubit behaviors relevant to networking components. These sandboxes provide practical exposure without the physical constraints or costs of hardware. Importantly, they foster a vibrant culture of experimentation where theories transform into testable models, accelerating learning and innovation within a supportive, low-barrier context.

Open-Source Projects

Harnessing the power of community, numerous open-source initiatives invite collaborators to build and improve quantum Internet software stacks and tools. SimulaQron and QuNetSim exemplify such projects, designed specifically to emulate quantum network nodes and protocols in accessible programming environments. SimulaQron allows users to simulate a quantum Internet by connecting multiple virtual quantum computers, facilitating distributed quantum algorithm testing and network protocol development.

QuNetSim extends this by providing a platform that mimics quantum network communication seamlessly integrated with classical control layers, enabling prototype design and performance evaluation. These projects thrive on contributions spanning code development, documentation, and testing, embracing newcomers who bring fresh perspectives. Participation here not only sharpens coding and protocol design skills but also places contributors at the heart of the quantum Internet's evolving infrastructure.

Standards and Working Group Participation

As the quantum Internet moves beyond laboratories into practical deployment, the establishment of standards becomes critical for interoperability, security, and scalability. Joining standardization efforts within organizations such as the European Telecommunications Standards Institute (ETSI), International Telecommunication Union (ITU), and the Institute of Electrical and Electronics Engineers (IEEE) offers a powerful venue for influencing the ecosystem's future design.

The Quantum Internet Alliance, along with other consortia, convenes working groups concentrating on topics from quantum key distribution protocols to hardware interfacing and network architecture. Through participation, contributors engage with a diverse mix of researchers, industry leaders, and policymakers, shaping guidelines that ensure different quantum networks can communicate and coexist harmoniously. Whether your expertise lies in policy, engineering, or theoretical modeling, these groups provide a platform to champion ideas and stay at the cutting edge of global collaboration.

Conferences and Workshops

Immersing yourself in the vibrant community of
quantum networking means frequenting its intellectual
crossroads: conferences and workshops. Events such
as the IEEE International Conference on Quantum
Computing and Engineering (QCE), Quantum Internet
and Network workshops, and the APS March Meeting
regularly congregate pioneers, early adopters, and
emerging talent. These gatherings serve multiple
roles—showcasing breakthrough research, unveiling
technological advancements, and fostering dialogues
between academia, industry, and government.

Presentations and posters give participants a platform
to share fresh insights, while informal networking
cultivates partnerships and mentorships that extend
beyond the event itself. Workshops, often more
interactive and focused, provide hands-on opportunities
to tackle practical challenges like protocol optimization
or quantum error correction. Engaging at these
venues enriches knowledge, sparks inspiration, and
builds a supportive network crucial for navigating and
contributing to the quantum Internet's rapid evolution.

Hackathons and Challenges

For those energized by time-bound, goal-oriented
collaboration, hackathons and challenge competitions
offer a rewarding path into quantum Internet
development. Events organized by academic groups,
industry players, and consortia provide high-intensity
environments where participants create prototypes of
quantum communication protocols, network simulators,
or cryptographic tools—often under 48 hours.

These competitive forums stimulate problem-solving
creativity while fostering teamwork across diverse
skill sets. Past challenges have driven innovations in

entanglement routing, quantum repeater efficiency, and user interface designs for quantum network control. Even for novices, hackathons yield valuable experiential learning and connections; for seasoned participants, they become a proving ground for new concepts and a showcase for skill.

Research Collaborations

Quantum networking's complexity demands the confluence of multiple disciplines and the pooling of resources—a fact well recognized by multi-institution collaborations and public-private partnerships. Universities, research laboratories, and industry leaders often form consortia aimed at pioneering specific quantum Internet components or applications. For example, the Quantum Flagship initiative in Europe and the United States National Quantum Initiative foster collaborations involving dozens of organizations.

Joining such efforts might entail becoming a student researcher in a university lab, contributing algorithms in a government-funded project, or consulting as part of an industrial partnership. These collaborative environments are fertile ground for learning, often providing access to rare hardware and expertise. They also underscore the communal nature of quantum Internet progress, illustrating that this transformative technology is the fruit of collective endeavor rather than solitary research.

Internships and Fellowships

Gaining practical experience at the intersection of theory and application is facilitated by internships and fellowship programs offered by quantum hardware manufacturers, software developers, service providers, and national laboratories. Companies like IBM, Google, and Rigetti maintain active quantum teams that welcome in-

281

terns across engineering, physics, and computer science disciplines.

Fellowship opportunities also abound in universities and research institutes, often supporting extended periods of study and innovation within quantum communication projects. These programs not only provide exposure to cutting-edge quantum devices and software stacks but also immerse participants in professional environments where networking, mentorship, and career development naturally unfold. For many, such experiential pathways are pivotal in transforming abstract knowledge into impactful real-world contributions.

Community Forums and Discussion Groups

The quantum Internet community thrives on dialogue, and digital platforms are its beating heart. Online forums such as the Quantum Computing Stack Exchange, research group mailing lists, and dedicated Discord or Slack channels facilitate vibrant discussions ranging from conceptual questions to troubleshooting technical hurdles.

These venues offer instant access to peer support, fostering collaborative problem-solving and the exchange of resources like tutorials, code snippets, and research papers. Regular participation can demystify complexities and accelerate learning, helping newcomers avoid common pitfalls and seasoned developers refine their approaches. Moreover, they function as informal networks that often catalyze project partnerships, hackathon teams, or joint publications.

Volunteer and Outreach Opportunities

Engagement with the quantum Internet extends beyond research and development; the community actively encourages outreach to broaden awareness and inclusivity. Volunteers contribute by organizing science communication events, developing educational materials, and supporting initiatives aimed at increasing diversity in quantum technology fields.

Programs focused on mentoring underrepresented groups or hosting public lectures build a more robust and equitable quantum Internet ecosystem. Such outreach nurtures the next generation of innovators and ensures that the benefits of quantum connectivity are distributed widely. Whether through local science fairs, online webinars, or school workshops, these volunteer activities enrich both participants and the broader community, making the quantum Internet not just an advanced technology but a shared human endeavor.

Engaging with the Quantum Internet Revolution

Becoming part of the quantum Internet landscape means stepping into a world where foundational science meets applied technology and global collaboration. Educational resources provide the scaffolding, while simulations and open-source projects offer playgrounds for creativity and experimentation. Participation in standards committees, conferences, and hackathons further hones expertise and expands networks. Practical experience gained through research collaborations, internships, and fellowships cultivates skills directly applicable to ongoing advancements.

Transcending technical engagement, community forums and outreach programs ensure that this revolution is participatory, inclusive, and vibrant. Whether you are a student, professional, or passionate curious bystander, numerous pathways exist to contribute to shaping a future where information flows with unprecedented security, speed, and capability. The quantum Internet is still in its infancy—your involvement today could help define the communication backbone of tomorrow's world.